"This book is for parents, grandparents, and caring friends who are faced with the challenges of an autistic child. You need not walk alone. Lynda Young brings you the benefit of hearing the voices of others who have walked this road, as well as professionals in the field. It is truly a book of hope and help."

—**Gary Chapman**, PhD, author of *The Five Love languages and Love as a Way of Life*

"As a parent and grandparent of children on the Autistic Spectrum, I know firsthand that whether the child joins your family by birth, foster care, or adoption, you feel as if the floor beneath you gave way and you are falling towards a crash landing. With its gentle, homey style, *Hope for Families of Children on the Autistic Spectrum* provides the soft landing caregivers need. Designed to be read a paragraph, page, or chapter at a time, this book is chock full of practical information interwoven with real-life stories. It will be dog-eared, tea-stained, and never out of sight. This as a gift, not only to new parents, but to the grandparents, aunties, and close friends who will interact with our Spectrum Children."

—**Sue Badeau**, speaker, writer, trainer, consultant; Adoptive and Foster Parent (and grandparent!); Director of Knowledge Management at Casey Family Programs; Senior Fellow, US Department of Justice, Office of Juvenile Justice and Delinquency Prevention

"*Hope for Families with Children on the Autistic Spectrum* is a fascinating book which will speak to the hearts of those parents, grandparents, and family members who have a child in their home with any degree of autism or spectrum disorders. Lynda provides specific examples—written by those who speak out of personal experience—and then makes suggestions for handling typical challenges on various developmental levels. Not only does she address the needs of children/teens with various spectrum disorders, but she gives advice to those who can provide help for the caregiver. Each chapter provides sound advice and encouragement from the Creator by citing specific biblical passages to be read and held as the source of all hope."

—**Marcia McQuitty**, Professor of Childhood Education Human Growth Division | School of Church and Family Ministries, Southwestern Baptist Theological Seminary

"If you have ever felt overwhelmed, isolated, or alone as a parent or educator of a child who is on the Autistic Spectrum, then this is the book for you. Lynda Young offers comfort, support, and resources to help you understand children on the spectrum, while also showing how God is with you every step of the way and that you are not alone."

—**Vicki Aiken**, proud parent of a successful adult child with Asperger's Syndrome; holds degrees in Early Childhood Education, Elementary Education Reading and Literacy, and certifications in special education, early childhood education, and gifted education

"Autism is difficult to understand, diverse in expression, and usually abounding with anguish. Countless books about the developmental, invisible diagnosis of autism can be put in categories: excellent information, or the expression of a personal journey, or alternative therapies, or blaming something or someone, or how to fix the problems, or. . . . However, this work stands alone because it is saturated with hope. Lynda is acutely informed, her writing is psychologically sound, and her expression is tender and simple. *Hope for Families of Children on the Autistic Spectrum* is saturated with hope. It resounds off of every page. I promise each reader, this book will change your life!"

—**Colleen Swindoll-Thompson** Disability Director of Insight for Living

"As a chronically ill mom with a son who has ADHD and SPD, *Hope for Families of Children on the Autistic Spectrum* shines a new light of encouragement. This book will help you feel as though a friend is alongside you for the journey— for the days you are exhausted and the moments of joyful discovery you see revealed in your child."

—**Lisa Copen**, founder of Rest Ministries for the chronically ill, and author of *Beyond Casseroles: 505 Ways to Encourage a Chronically Ill Friend*

Hope

for Families of
Children on the
Autistic Spectrum

Hope

for Families of Children on the Autistic Spectrum

Lynda T. Young

LEAFWOOD
PUBLISHERS

HOPE FOR FAMILIES OF CHILDREN ON THE AUTISTIC SPECTRUM

LEAFWOOD
P U B L I S H E R S

Copyright 2011 by Lynda T. Young

ISBN 978-0-89112-297-5
LCCN 2011038947

Printed in the United States of America

Scripture quotations, unless otherwise noted, are from The Holy Bible, New International Version. Copyright 1984, International Bible Society. Used by permission of Zondervan Publishers. Scripture quotations noted MSG taken from *The Message*. Copyright 1993, 1994, 1995, 1996, 2000, 2001, 2002. Used by permission of NavPress Publishing Group. Scripture quotations noted NLT are taken from the Holy Bible, New Living Translation, copyright 1996, 2004. Used by permission of Tyndale House Publishers, Inc., Wheaton, Illinois 60189. All rights reserved. Scripture noted NKJV taken from the New King James Version. Copyright © 1982 by Thomas Nelson, Inc. Used by permission. All rights reserved.

PERMISSIONS:
"Welcome to Holland," ©1987 by Emily Perl Kingsley. All rights reserved. Reprinted by permission of the author.

Story taken from *Dancing with Max* by Charles W. Colson; Emily Colson Boehme. Copyright © 2011 by Emily Colson Boehme and Charles W. Colson . Used by permission of Zondervan.

A Beautiful Once, used by permission of Anna Geary.

Poem by Tim Tucker, used by permission of Tim Tucker (www.bothhandsandaflashlight.com).

Colleen Swindoll-Thompson, story from her blog at Insight.org, permission granted.

LIBRARY OF CONGRESS CATALOGING-IN-PUBLICATION DATA
Young, Lynda T.
Hope for families of children on the autistic spectrum / Lynda T. Young.
    p. cm.
ISBN 978-0-89112-297-5
1. Parents of developmentally disabled children--Religious life. 2. Autism spectrum disorders--Religious aspects--Christianity. 3. Children with autism spectrum disorders--Care. I. Title.
BV4596.P35Y68 2011
248.8'45--dc23

                                                                    2011038947

Cover design by ThinkPen Design, LLC | Interior text design by Sandy Armstrong

Leafwood Publishers is an imprint of Abilene Christian University Press
1626 Campus Court | Abilene, Texas 79601

1-877-816-4455 | www.leafwoodpublishers.com

                    11 12 13 14 15 16 / 7 6 5 4 3 2 1

Dedication

*To the members of our family who've been affected
by the spectrum—I've seen the reality of this
journey lived out in the lives of the parents and
other family members. They have inspired me.*

*To my husband, John, who has given me
total support in the You Are Not Alone book
series journey—and in everything else in life.*

*To the families (readers) on your challenging
journey, and all the "come-alongsiders"—
friends and professionals whose encouragement
brings a shining ray of hope on dark days.*

*To those who've prayed through the writing of
this book and prayed for those who'll read it.
Only in heaven will all those prayers be known.*

Contents

God's "Coincidence"

Twenty-five years ago, in Maryland, a small writer's group met in Lois's home once a week for a year. During that time, I met her teenaged daughter, Chris. Fast-forward to 2011—I reconnected with Lois through Facebook, where I told her I was writing a book on autism. She mentioned that Chris was now a speech-language pathologist, had worked with special needs children for twenty years—many on the autistic spectrum—and then added, "Maybe you'd like to contact her."

I did, and during the final three weeks of my work on this book, Chris came alongside and shared her wealth of knowledge, her compassion for her clients, and her love for our Lord. She's added the "salt," preparing the book for you, the readers. God's "coincidence," indeed.

Also, thank you to those who provided proofreading and encouragement during the writing process. You know who you are, and so does our Lord. You've done eternity's work.

Mainly, thank you to the One our hope is in.

Foreword

Kate, my eight-year-old Asperger's child, and I were sitting, waiting for Adam, my ten-year-old son, at rehearsal. It was getting boring. The rehearsal was running long, we were hungry, and we were sitting on the hard, cold floor of the hallway. We'd run through our bag of books and artwork. Kate was starting to get disgruntled, and she was becoming disruptive. Next to us were two little girls working on something. I surreptitiously leaned closer. It was complicated music notation, or at least complicated for their age. I asked them what grade they were in—they answered, "first." I looked at my third grade Kate, who could barely make it through a day of school, let alone music lessons, and inwardly sighed. I got out my iPad and booted up a fun game called "Toontastic." This game allows you to make your own cartoon videos, with you as the voice-over artist. Kate eagerly started working on a new video. I noticed the first grade girls looking sideways at Kate, curiously. Soon they were edging closer. Kate asked if they wanted to join her in making a movie, and before long all three girls were making a cartoon and giggling hilariously—the music notation and cold floor forgotten. I put my head back against the wall and took a deep breath, happy for a moment to close my eyes and relax my vigilance. My daughter may be slightly "weird" (her own word), she may not be able to concentrate on schoolwork, but by golly, she can make friends. Thank you, God.

Life with an Autistic Spectrum Disorder (ASD) child is like this. One moment it's meltdowns and attitude, and the next, cuddles and laughs. You just never know what's going to happen next. When you're new to the diagnosis, it can feel pretty overwhelming. Information is coming thick and fast, advice flying past you like some strange "Matrix" dream, and it's hard to catch or hold on to any of it. Where could I find some peace, some respite from the information bullet train?

Lynda's book is exactly that: a restful breath in the midst of chaos. She gives us some most welcome suggestions and help. But more than that, she reminds us to seek God's peace in the funnel cloud of our external situation. Her advice is constantly tempered with Scripture, enriched by the Word of God. God knows exactly where we are in our journey and wants nothing so much as to hold us and give us his peace.

Seven years ago, when my son was diagnosed with leukemia, I would blog about it in order to make some sense of it. An old classmate of mine showed my blog to Lynda, who was, at the time, working on a book for parents of kids with cancer. Isn't it awesome how God works? Lynda and I struck up a friendship through e-mails and scattered phone calls, and I was so blessed to be a part of her book about cancer.

Two years later, my daughter was diagnosed with autism, and again God's timing was amazing, because Lynda was starting to think about her next book—the one that you are holding in your hands today. Though we have never met in person, a country between us, Lynda is a constant support to me. I don't blog as much anymore, but we keep in touch through social networking, where I frequently post about what life is like with a spectrum child. Lynda is my staunchest ally, lifting me and my family up in prayer, reminding me what I'm doing right, and encouraging me when times get tough. I am so thankful that God connected us.

The book that you are holding in your hands is a lot like that: Lynda wrote it just for you. She is upholding each of you in prayer, hoping to help you see the good in the diagnosis, and urging you to carry on the work God has given you. Because, you see, you have a job to do. *You* are the person God has entrusted with this unique, fascinating, frustrating enigma that is your atypical child. It's hard work, without question, but it's *good* work. *Hope for Families of Children on the Autistic Spectrum* is a handbook of joy, celebrating and praying with you as you continue your good work.

As the parent of an atypical child, my wish for you is a moment of peace in what may seem like a cold, hard hallway ahead. You are not alone, and you are not without help.

Meanwhile, the moment we get tired in the waiting, God's Spirit is right alongside helping us along. If we don't know how or what to pray, it doesn't matter. He does our praying in and for us, making prayer out of our wordless sighs, our aching groans. He knows us far better than we know ourselves, knows our [encumbered] condition, and keeps us present before God. That's why we can be so sure that every detail in our lives of love for God is worked into something good.

—Romans 8:26-28 MSG

Elizabeth Boegel
Walnut Creek, California

The "Alphabet" Soup

Lean your face close to a hot bowl of soup with starchy letters floating on top. Your glasses steam up as you breathe in the spicy vegetable smells. Now, dip your spoon into the soup, stir, and capture the vegetables, broth, and letters. Slowly slurp the soup and taste the goodness. Mmm. This is one kind of alphabet soup—a delicious one, comforting and soothing.

But there's another alphabet soup chocked full of letters, and it's not so soothing. Many parents say, "My child is an 'alphabet' soup child—diagnosed with so many letters [initials]. How do we even know which ones are valid?"

It seems new information, websites, and opinions pop up every day. Symptoms can mesh with one another, overlap, be caused by the same brain disorder, not be caused by the same brain disorder, be caused by something else that no one can figure out—ASD, ADD, ADHD, SPD, NLD—and the list goes on and on.

"We need all the information, testing, and help we can get," a dad said. "It's like we're stumbling through a fog."

Remember, you know your child best and you are your child's best advocate—even if you have trouble communicating and relating to him or her at times. You've studied the "soup," but you struggle with making words out of the letters floating around.

The letters are elusive, at times clearly visible—yet why do they look so different from one minute to the next? And there are always a few we miss at the bottom of the bowl, things we just couldn't catch with our spoon.

We're introducing you to other families who've traveled your journey, as well as professionals who come alongside to encourage you through stories, helpful hints, and resources—all to bring you hope. You are not alone.

At the end of each chapter in this book, you'll find letters floating in your "spoon" as you dip into your bowl of alphabet soup. May the words penned by King David in the Old Testament bring comfort and hope for your journey, as you look to the One whom the hope is in—the Shepherd. Some verses will be divided, so they will have both "a" and "b" parts.

Psalm 23 NLT

A psalm of David

[1] The LORD is my shepherd;
    I have all that I need.
[2] He lets me rest in green meadows;
    he leads me beside peaceful streams.
    [3] He renews my strength.
He guides me along right paths,
    bringing honor to his name.
[4] Even when I walk
    through the darkest valley,
I will not be afraid,
    for you are close beside me.
Your rod and your staff
    protect and comfort me.
[5] You prepare a feast for me
    in the presence of my enemies.
You honor me by anointing my head with oil.
    My cup overflows with blessings.
[6] Surely your goodness and unfailing love will
pursue me
    all the days of my life,
    and I will live in the house of the LORD
        forever.

"Welcome To Holland"

By Emily Perl Kingsley

I am often asked to describe the experience of raising a child with a disability—to try to help people who have not shared that unique experience to understand it, to imagine how it would feel. It's like this . . .

When you're going to have a baby, it's like planning a fabulous vacation trip—to Italy. You buy a bunch of guide books and make your wonderful plans. The Coliseum. Michelangelo's *David*. The gondolas in Venice. You may learn some handy phrases in Italian. It's all very exciting.

After months of eager anticipation, the day finally arrives. You pack your bags and off you go. Several hours later, the plane lands. The flight attendant comes in and says, "Welcome to Holland."

"Holland?!?" you say. "What do you mean Holland?? I signed up for Italy! I'm supposed to be in Italy. All my life I've dreamed of going to Italy."

But there's been a change in the flight plan. They've landed in Holland and there you must stay.

The important thing is that they haven't taken you to a horrible, disgusting, filthy place full of pestilence, famine, and disease. It's just a different place.

So you must go out and buy new guide books. And you must learn a whole new language. And you will meet a whole new group of people you never would have met.

It's just a *different* place. It's slower-paced than Italy, less flashy than Italy. But after you've been there for a while and you catch your breath, you look around . . . and you begin to notice that Holland has windmills . . . and Holland has tulips. Holland even has Rembrandts.

But everyone you know is busy coming and going from Italy . . . and they're all bragging about what a wonderful time they had there. And for the rest of your life, you will say, "Yes, that's where I was supposed to go. That's what I had planned."

And the pain of that will never, ever, ever, ever go away . . . because the loss of that dream is a very, very significant loss.

But . . . if you spend your life mourning the fact that you didn't get to Italy, you may never be free to enjoy the very special, the very lovely things about Holland.

Chapter One

What's the Spectrum (And Who Is on It?)

*Trust in the LORD with all your heart, and lean
not on your own understanding. In all your ways
acknowledge him, and he will make your path straight.*

—Proverbs 3:5–6
(The favorite verse of a mom on the ASD journey)

Thank you for taking the time to open this book and read. I know some days you don't have time to brush your teeth, much less sit and read, so—read at your leisure. "Leisure?" you say. Well, when you *do* have a few minutes, grab a cup of coffee and read a page or two. Feel free to mark it up; write notes in the margins. Make it yours. It was written for you.

Here's the code describing children that we'll use throughout the book:

- SC (spectrum child)
- TC (typical child—one who doesn't fall on the spectrum. Notice that I didn't say "normal" child—what makes any of us "normal"?)

Your SC may or may not fit the stories shared in this book. The helpful hints that are given may dovetail with what you've done already, may be ideas to try, or may not be what you need. The variables on this journey are mind boggling and we can't cover all situations. So, take what you can use, and put the other information aside—maybe you can share it with someone who needs it on their unique journey.

ASD: Autistic Spectrum Disorder

Some Family Gene Pools

"When we read the diagnosis criteria for our child Blaine, it hit me—some of those behaviors describe me!" Frank said.

"It explains a lot about Frank over the years," his wife, Dorren, said, and she winked at Frank.

Frank shook his head and continued. "We also realized why we struggled with the behaviors in our other children, just not as severe as Blaine's. With the information and help we're receiving, Blaine's future is going to be so different than two years ago when we were totally in the dark—and we're getting a handle on our other children's uniqueness too. It certainly benefits the whole family."

The result of a diagnosis and the education that follows: we understand the reasons why the other family members we love act the way they do. The ongoing journey needs as much information and inspiration as possible.

The Spectrum

As I drove over the crest of the hill, cars were pulled over to the side of the road. People stood outside and looked at the sky, as they snapped pictures with their iPhones and other gadgets.

> If you've met one child on the spectrum, you've met one child on the spectrum. They're all different.

Then I saw it. The crystal-clear colors arched across the horizon—a magnificent rainbow. It took my breath away. The different shades and hues, varied degrees of intensity, some barely visible (indigo), others vibrant, but together they melded into a breathtaking rainbow—a spectrum of color.

There's another spectrum with different degrees of intensity, some subtle, some more obvious. These are children (and adults) on the Autistic Spectrum. Some carry different diagnoses, some no diagnosis, and some fall under many labels. The following questions and statement from parents are common:

- "Does he have ADHD?"
- "How is PDD/NOS different from Asperger's?"
- "I don't really want a diagnosis at all—at least not right now."

If a child has a *pervasive* (interferes and affects parts of their life) challenge, then he may be on the spectrum. If he has symptoms inconsistent with his developmental level, he may be on the spectrum. But realize everyone is unique; we meld together in the rainbow of humanity, and all are needed and valuable.

"When my son hugged me for the first time, it took my breath away," a mom said.

Your child on the *spectrum* can take your breath away.

What is the spectrum?

Umbrella term: Autism is an umbrella term for a wide spectrum of disorders referred to as Pervasive Developmental Disorders (PDD) or Autism Spectrum Disorders (ASD).

Which is which? ASD and PPD are used interchangeably.

Why a spectrum? Wide range of intensity, symptoms and behaviors, types of disorders, and considerable individual variation.

One end of spectrum? Children with ASD may have a striking lack of interest and ability to interact, limited ability to communicate, and show repetitive behaviors and distress over changes, as in the case of many with classic autism, or Autistic Disorder.

Other end of spectrum? Children with a high-functioning form of autism who may have unusual social, language, and play skills, as in Asperger Syndrome.

What disorders are officially listed on the spectrum? The autistic spectrum consists of the following disorders: Autistic Disorder or Classic Autism, Rett's Disorder or Rett Syndrome, Childhood Disintegrative Disorder, Asperger's Disorder or Asperger Syndrome, Pervasive Developmental Disorder—Not Otherwise Specified (PDD-NOS)

How does the spectrum brain work? They're a group of *neurobiological* disorders that affect a child's ability to interact, communicate, relate, play, imagine, and learn.

What else may be spectrum related? Immunological, gastrointestinal, and metabolic problems.

When can you see signs and symptoms? Seen in early childhood—as early as ten months.

New Jargon

If your child is anywhere on the spectrum, your vocabulary is crammed with new jargon—and some of it includes initials. (See Glossary for more terms and definitions.)

- ODD: Oppositional Defiance Disorder
- OCD: Obsessive Compulsive Disorder
- SPD: Sensory Processing Disorder
- ASD: Autistic Spectrum Disorder
- ADD: Attention Deficit Disorder
- ADHD: Attention Deficit Hyperactivity Disorder
- PDD: Pervasive Development Disorder
- PDD/NOS: Pervasive Development Disorder/Not Otherwise Specified

"As a baby, Vance ran laps in his crib, and still can outrun and outlast anyone his age. It's exhausting for me, and our pediatrician says he has ADHD. Is that on the spectrum?" a mom asked.

"Danielle makes fair grades, but her teacher, Mrs. Soloman, says she mainly stares out the window—and when she calls her name, she says, 'Huh?' Mrs. Soloman thinks we need to have her checked for ADD. Is that on the spectrum?"

Some professionals don't list ADHD and ADD on the spectrum—others do. Professionals' opinions vary. Parents' opinions vary. People (who never slow down or stare into space), their opinions vary also.

"It is what it is," say some professionals, "and we treat the symptoms if they interfere with the patient's life—depending on how severe the symptoms are."

"Our child was tested by two highly qualified professionals and we were given two different diagnoses."

"We've learned a whole new language in a short time—rapid–fire information. The words help, but we're still walking through a fog."

Professionals You May Meet on the Journey

Meet the professionals—remember they are human first and professionals second. They have different personalities (see Resource One) just like you, and they deal with their own family's health issues, challenges with children at home, elderly parents, and the shaky economy, but they have chosen to share *your* spectrum world. In that world, they cope with crises, walk a tightrope between empathizing with you and your child and being a detached professional that tries not to carry everyone's problems, becoming ineffective as a result.

> There isn't a "one stop shop" for a professional to globally analyze all the components you need for your child.

> Professionals are human first and professionals second.

Parents and professionals, beware of "compassion fatigue." It can hit and overwhelm anyone, and it happens when someone cares too much about a situation. Yes, we can care too much; we know compassion fatigue has hit when our caring becomes counterproductive and we become ineffective. More on this subject in Chapter Eight, Caring for the Caregiver.

"Our life is full of '-ists' and '-gists', and we're thankful for their help," a mom said.

Turn to Resource Two to find out what they do—you need to know the scopes of each of their practices—and how it compliments or conflicts with the other professionals on your journey:

- Allergists
- Behaviorists
- Child Life Specialists
- Counselors
- Educational: Teachers,
  Teacher's Aides, Bus Drivers
- Neuropsychiatrists
- Nutritionists
- Occupational Therapists
- Pediatricians
- Physical Therapists
- Psychiatrists
- Psychologists
- Social Workers
- Speech Therapists
- . . . and anyone who comes alongside you and your child.

Who do you listen to? Have you gotten differing opinions from professionals who've evaluated your child, and from others who have very different opinions about what you should and should not do to help your child—and now you're trying to decide what compliments or conflicts with their individual opinions? All are trying to help with the same problem, but they may have widely varied backgrounds and experiences. Consider what they say, and see how it stacks up with what you know about your child.

Trading Places

It's interesting to watch two characters in a movie who've "traded places." This is usually done without their consent, and each feels uncomfortable. But as the plot continues, they gain a realization of how the other feels as they react and interact with the world around them.

If you traded places with your child for a day, you'd have a glimpse into his or her world—a perspective only he has seen or experienced. Your child can't tell you or explain his or her unique point of view and reactions to the world, so, for the first time, you'd be able to experience your child's world.

> April is Autism Awareness Month.

If that day in your child's skin included a meltdown, you'd *understand* the eruption over the *wrong* cereal waiting for him at breakfast (never mind that the favorite kind was totally consumed yesterday). You would simply be overwhelmed by a tidal wave of frustration and anger. That's just how it is—how your child's brain is wired.

Well, you can't trade places (even though you'd really love for your child to experience your go-with-the-flow—or so you think—personality) for a day. The following is the next best solution to assist you in identifying with your child.

What is a situation that upsets you and makes you feel totally out of control? Let's say it's fear of enclosed places—like a shed in your backyard. You step in to grab a gardening tool, and the wind blows the door shut. It's totally dark, your heart starts racing, and you frantically search for the door. Your hand gropes down the door for the knob. As you turn the knob—it won't move. All of a sudden you can't breathe (so your emotions scream at you), and you bang on the door while sweat runs down your face and your heart races. You scream for help and your mind knows someone will hear you, but your emotions override your head. How do you feel? Hold that thought.

> There's a reason your child melted down—changes in routine or transitions—they make sense—but he can't tell you with language or appropriate body language.

Switch to the morning your daughter, Anna, wanted to wear her yellow sundress (the tags removed, of course) and her flip flops. A storm had moved in the night before, and the temperature plunged to thirty-three degrees. The wind continued to rattle the windows as you finished preparing breakfast. And now here she stands, ready for school in her yellow sundress and flip flops. You had planned ahead knowing the battle that would ensue. You had her winter coat laid out. She glances at the coat lying across the chair and states, "I'm not wearing that."

You take a breath and answer in your most calm voice, "It's really cold out, and you'll need it."

"I don't care."

Voices grow louder, breakfast is a moot point, and the meltdown hits full force.

Anna's heart races, sweat pours down her face, and she struggles to breathe. She has no control over the screaming emotions and effects.

Sound familiar? It doesn't make sense to you that she's melting down about having to wear a coat on a cold day (even over her favorite dress, never mind the flip flops); just like it didn't make sense to think you'd never get out of the dark shed with the stuck doorknob. Our emotions don't make sense at times, but they give us a small understanding when we attempt to trade places with a person in an overwhelmed state.

Unfortunately, your child may experience tidal waves of emotion bombarding her many times during the day, depending on the circumstances. As you learn her triggers, more can be done by planning ahead and taking deep breaths yourself.

The characters in the movie struggled with the changes they faced in their new identities, but they usually came to appreciate the other's walk in life. You can't trade places with your child, but can choose to appreciate their unique walk in life as you give unconditional love and pray for understanding. There may come a time when your child turns to you and says, "Are you sad today?" Indeed, a "trading places" occurred, and you're overwhelmed with the thought, "She understood my feelings."

> Knowledge is power to overcome and deal with problems.

As you read this book, my desire is to bring hope to you on your journey—and not to add frustration. Each child is unique, and each family is unique. As you read others' stories, I pray that some information will cause an "Aha! That's why she does that," moment for you. I pray that as you realize you aren't alone, you'll receive inspiration and spiritual strength for your journey—and wisdom to do the next right thing.

Letters floating in your spoon:

S-H-E-P-H-E-R-D

The LORD is my shepherd; I have all that I need.

—Psalm 23:1 NLT

Chapter Two

"I'm Sorry to Tell You . . ."

I believe in the sun when it is not shining. I believe in love when I feel it not. I believe in God even when He is silent.

—Words found written on a cellar
wall in Cologne after World War II.

Your New Normal

Were you thrust unexpectedly into the spectrum world, or did you know something just *wasn't right*? Did you deny obvious signs that needed to be addressed, avoiding a diagnosis, or did you beg for one? Wherever you've been on your journey and the steps you've taken, you're probably now in the *new normal* of your life. Things were normal, then your world exploded when you heard, "I'm sorry to tell you, but your child is . . . ," and now you're adjusting to that new normal.

How do you handle it? Some parents who share their stories, books, and blogs write about their young adult "child" whom they love. They describe how that child brings them such joy. And that child does. But here you are, struggling on your journey. If you didn't know their complete story you might conclude that every challenge had been simple to accept—the right treatments were easily found and were free or inexpensive, siblings adjusted beautifully, the parents were always of one mind about how the child would be disciplined, educated, and nurtured, and everyone lived happily ever after.

> "When a train goes through a tunnel and it gets dark, you don't throw away the ticket and jump off. You sit still and trust the engineer."
>
> —Corrie ten Boom

Those "once upon a time" stories are stories. Parents do love their children, and want the best for their lives. But, no, it isn't easy. It isn't inexpensive (usually), the siblings would like more of their parents' time and attention, and parents struggle with decisions (major and minor ones) dealing with their family.

I had a kindergarten student who began each made-up story with "Ponce upon a time . . ." It took me awhile to figure out what she was saying. That's how *she'd* heard "Once upon a time," and she ended every story with "they lived happily ever after amen."

Communication with Anyone in the House

Every family has a story, their "once upon a time," but lots of things happen before "amen." Families need extra help, especially to deal with empty emotional tanks drained daily from stress. Take a few minutes to flip to the back of the book, Resource One, the You-niquely Made Personality Study, to discover why we act as we do—and especially why others act as they do. We need all the help we can get to *fill* those empty emotional tanks.

Autistic Spectrum Disorders (ASDs) change the dynamics of the family. All members are still who they are, but their personalities become intensified from the stress. Weaknesses become more obvious, and strengths are often taken to the extreme in an attempt to cope.

Some parents spend endless hours foraging for information on every spectrum website, and then trace every link that appears. That parent will be a wealth of needed information on this journey, but they may not realize how they have cut off face to face communication with their spouse. Conversely, their spouse (usually the opposite personality) could care less about the internet

> "Even good things can be overdone."

38

and craves hugs, snuggling, and a shoulder to cry on. Different needs, different emotional tanks to be filled—*differently.*

Roles

Mom may spend most of her time and energy absorbed in the care of their SC. She doesn't have much left over for her husband when he comes in the door, and she would relish time by herself to regroup. "If my husband would just take over now until bedtime. . . ." Then reality hits. Her evening won't include her daydream. The result: very little connection with her husband, for the rest of the evening.

Dad comes home and wants more than anything a smile from his son, and a hug. But that smile and hug may not happen, and he watches his son turn away and concentrate on playing with his favorite inanimate object. His son doesn't acknowledge his dad is even there. The result: no connection.

"All we talk about is autism—and what he's done, not done, treatment plans, finances, all dealing with autism. Our world," one dad says. "When you don't connect with people in your family, you feel like the outsider. You know it's a struggle for everyone, but slowly you drift away—and some men simply leave. They don't think anyone really cares if they're there, and they don't feel like they make any contribution (except financially) to the family—the family they are supposed to be taking care of. They feel guilty, but just escape."

"I want to talk about my frustrations with my husband, and I want to say, 'Just let me talk, don't try to fix it. You can't. Just let me vent.'"

Forewarned is forearmed. Knowing the pitfalls ahead, you can schedule strategies for strengthening your marriage. Discover more about personalities, how you've dealt with struggles in the past, and your

> Others reactions may not make sense to you, but they do (in some way) make sense to them.

"love language" (see Resource One). All play a huge part in how you will handle this journey.

Schedule Strategies for Your Journey

Division of Labor

How do you divide the labor? Who is the most able to do what? Is mom better at keeping records and details? Is dad better at coping with bedtime rituals? Is mom a morning person and can handle getting the child up, getting the child dressed, getting the child to eat breakfast, getting the child to school? Is dad a night person who can fend off meltdowns while helping with homework, getting the child to take a shower or bath, dealing with the toys placed in certain rows on the bed, reading stories in a certain order, turning lights off or on? (It's exhausting to think of any of those responsibilities.) Determining who is able to to what better will give you a starting point on dividing the labor.

> Bonding between parents, and between parents and child, comes with time, patience, practice (consistency), and prayer.

First, write down a typical day in a notebook (see Glossary), which includes things to be done in a week or in a month. Also, keep track of finances, down time for each parent, and down time together. A notebook with those sections is a great place to start (and continue updating). Things will change from time to time (maybe hour to hour), and the issues you had last week may be completely different this week. The strategies you planned (and, hopefully, carried out) may or may not work the next week. *Try* to stay flexible.

Successes

The successes you've had in certain areas (for instance, how you got your child to brush his or her teeth before going to school—when you thought all your child's teeth would rot and fall out before you finally *forced* him to put the brush in his mouth) are almost forgotten until you look back at previous journal entries. "Oh, yeah, that was a huge struggle." It helps you appreciate where you've come from. Each step forward is a giant leap. Take time to appreciate it.

Issues

Do you have an issue (a nice word for "problem") this week that you've been tackling for months? It's time to check in with someone for extra advice, or help of some kind. When you've been in the battle for a long time, you lose perspective, and if you keep doing the same thing with the same results, it's time for a change. When someone suggests a different strategy, don't roll your eyes and say, "We've tried that before and it didn't work." You may have tried it before and it didn't work, but it may be time to try it again (your child and you are changing), and it may just need to be tweaked some.

For example: Your child refuses to do what you've asked—so, have you tried these suggestions? Give her a specific time when she has to get up, and set an alarm on a clock—when that goes off, that's it. If she still refuses, take away an item she *wants*. In doing so, use a calmer voice, or have another family member be the one to tell her to do something. Write any suggestions and things you've tried or heard in the notebook under Helpful Hints, and go back over what's worked and what hasn't (and why). This is so valuable to your family's well-being, and it provides information to others involved in your child's life.

"I don't have to write it down, because I'm sure I'll remember these things," a mom said.

No, you probably won't. Your mind is packed, and it can only hold so much. Someone who isn't stressed will remember some things, but add stress

> "I'm sure I won't forget." Yes, you probably will.

on top, and that list of things you remember gets shorter. These types of hints will be crowded out of your brain. Having it on paper is a great reminder—and you don't have to spend the energy of trying to remember; the paper tells you what to do.

Your Personal Life

Another part of your life that needs attention is your sexual relationship.

"But I feel guilty seeking pleasure in the midst of all this," a mom said.

"Besides, I'm too exhausted," her husband added. "And I'm worn down worrying about finances. And I never even have time to shave."

Plan ahead and take the time needed to stay close and reassured of each other's love.

Single Caregivers

"At least she has a husband to help her," a single mom said. "Okay, I'm sorry—I'm venting." Venting is needed, especially when you're traveling this journey by yourself. How do you split the fragments of time—caregiver for your child, work (if that is even an option), spending time with your other child(ren)—and squeeze in a quick, hot shower to be able to go out in public—if you even have time to do that?

> Glossary Helps:
> Floortime

"Money is tight at the best, and now the added help for my child. It comes down to food on the table, or gas to get to appointments, or pay bills, or home therapies my child desperately needs. Other families are struggling also, we chat on the internet and swap helpful hints—the biggest help is knowing other singles are living the same life I am."

What if you're a grandmother who is raising a grandchild on the spectrum—along with other siblings? "I'm getting older and I'm even having trouble getting up and down off the floor with my grandson. 'Floortime,' they say?"

One of the biggest challenges is carrying the weight of family decisions. "Whose opinion do I ask for—my typical toddler or three-year-old, or my SC seven-year-old? I'd relish having other adults to bounce things off of."

A team approach relieves stress for the family, but when your team consists of only you and your young children, then you certainly need more help. The following suggestions are from others who have walked this journey as a single caregiver. Even though each family will have different dynamics and age groups, they still get it. The following suggestions help *all* families.

- Don't isolate yourself. This is, of course, easier said than done. You know if you get out in public with your child, chances are it won't be easy—but don't take the easier way and stay home all the time. Plan ahead for outings with your child, but also find someone (if at all possible) to take care of your child so that you can have an outing on your own. A resource person who can take your child overnight will give you the "rest" you need. Some single therapists who are certified in "respite care" may be able to do this over a weekend or in the summer.
- Keep up with a journal of your feelings, papers regarding your child, and a calendar (see Glossary).
- Establish consistent routines. Yes, your child has already established his routines, but establish them for you and the family also. Consistency gives a feeling of security for everyone.

> You can't be God for your child, but you can hand her over to him in prayer each day.

- Encourage consistent (there's that word again) discipline of your children. Work out a plan with someone who understands your journey. The discipline will vary from child to child in some ways, but it will set needed boundaries.
- Treat kids like kids, not as a substitute for an adult partner. It's easy to put the oldest child into an adult role when you're exhausted and need help.
- Keep communication lines open with others through the internet, Facebook, Twitter, and phone calls.

If you do nothing else each day, simply ask your spouse or others helping care for your child, "What is one thing I can do for you today?" That will shine a bright ray of hope into their life—and you'll be surprised how much you receive in doing so.

Letters floating in your spoon:
R - E - S - T

He lets me rest in green meadows.

—Psalm 23:2a NLT

Chapter Three

Caring for Your Unique Child

*Our main business is not to see what lies dimly in
the distance but to do clearly what lies at hand.*

—Thomas Carlyle

One Size Does Not Fit All

What do thumbprints, snowflakes, and children have in common? They're unique—no two thumbprints, snowflakes, or children are exactly the same. You can't be "sort of" unique, according to the dictionary's definition. Unique is absolute, and your child is absolutely him or herself—with a mixture of age, personality, and gene pool. If he fits somewhere on the spectrum, *multiple* variables are added.

> Everyone is uniquely made.

Simple as ABC

"Raising a child seems as simple as A-B-C," a mom of three typical children said. Her children were well behaved, obedient, talented, and smart—they didn't seem like *real* children, even in the world of "typical" children.

Another mom sitting nearby whispered, "My child isn't even close to being 'typical,' much less perfect—and raising him certainly isn't simple."

You may have heard simplistic answers from moms raising typical children, such as, "Your son will just outgrow that," or, "Good, strict discipline would take care of that." The "that" is your child's behavior, so be careful as others' words sink into your mind not to react (as much as possible). The moms usually mean well and don't want to hurt you, but they haven't walked in your shoes. Or they may be moms who *have* walked in your shoes, but they have strong opinions on the way you should be handling issues and making decisions (which would be *their* way).

Remember, you know your child better than anyone.

Step back and take a deep breath. When you are calm, take an objective look at these issues with your child. Objectivity seems like a steep hill, but how is your exchange of ideas, interaction, and contact with your child? What do you see or hear *from* your child? Your "hearing" may be in the form of careful behavioral observations that give you clues to what your child needs and wants.

When you begin to accept your child as he is—and then begin your first steps as his advocate—you're on your way. The following ABCs will help you on your journey with your child.

A: Accept and appreciate your child.

B: Believe in your child (encourage, not discourage).

C: Communicate with your child.

Accept and Appreciate

Accept and appreciate who she is. Make a list of her strengths, and write down her challenges. Be as objective as possible—and yes, she may outgrow some of the challenges, but for today, write what you see.

Believe

Believe in him. *All* children's emotional tanks need to be filled to give them courage on their journey through life, but spectrum children require more help along the way. They need tangible "reinforcers" (perhaps stickers), but they also need your words and your body language.

Here's what a spectrum child might be thinking as you encourage or discourage him with your words and body language.

Acts that Encourage:	Acts that Discourage:
Acknowledge his accomplishments: "Good job," (and mean it).	Camouflaging him: He'll assume he's not good enough.
Respect him: Honor his choices. He will know that you believe in him.	Pitying him: When you shake your head and say, "Bless your heart," you are hindering his emotional growth.
Listen to his chatter: Look him in the eye, smile, and talk to him face-to-face.	Ignoring his chatter or not looking at him: When you ignore him or just mumbling, "Uh huh," he'll realize what he says isn't important—and that he's not important.
Prepare him for changes: Tell him about holidays—get him ready step-by-step. He will feel involved.	Conceding: He will believe he's not worth the bother—it's overwhelming anyway.
Embrace him and who he is: In public, plan ahead and have answers for people—especially when you're tired. He will know he is accepted.	Reacting to others: When you lash out at other's insensitivity, he will believe that you are ashamed.
Support and foster: Hold on when needed; let go when it's time.	Hindering: Not holding on or not letting go when it is time.
Focus on him: If you're a Type A+, slow down and just be with him. He will know he's important.	Occupying yourself with other things: Keep going and don't slow down—if you stay busy, you won't have to deal with him as much. He will see that he is not worth your time.

Communicate

Communication is only a small percentage verbal, the rest is non-verbal (body language)—and your child may have trouble with both verbal and non-verbal communication.

Communication with typical children (TCs):

- If your child is physically sick, you take care of her physical needs and she understands why you are doing what you're doing to help.
- If she's unusually sad and withdrawn, you snuggle with her and ask her what's wrong.
- If she's angry, you tell her to shoot some hoops, and when she's worn out, you talk about what's wrong (if you're lucky).

> "Stims" or "stimming" are repetitious movements that are soothing for an SC.

That's communication (interaction) with a typical child who reacts typically to changes, transitions, disappointments, and life.

But what do you do if your child pulls away from hugs (and touches), turns her head so as not to meet your eyes, and retreats into her world of stims?

"He doesn't need me," a mom said. "I'm there for him, I reach out to him physically and emotionally—and he recoils as if I was going to harm him. How do I deal with that?"

Why doesn't your communication (verbal and non-verbal) connect with your SC? They hear your words, but the meaning doesn't register. It's as if you're speaking a foreign language to them: "Machai is so literal, everything is black or white;" or "Sunny hears a joke and her expression never changes—not even a smile cracked."

"My teen-aged son Kevin knows that jokes are supposed to be funny, and that other people will laugh, and that's a good thing, but when he tells a joke (that he's usually made up), people just stare at him. It's like listening to a five-year-old tell a 'Knock Knock' joke and only he knows why it's funny. Kevin never understands why *his* joke isn't funny, and kids don't laugh, and some end up making fun of him."

> *Behavior modification* affects your everyday life for everyone in your home—not just your child (see Glossary).

Over time, and with lots of follow through with behavior modification, behavior management, and other strategies, SC's actions may change, so don't give up.

Continue to use the ABCs daily with your child (and everyone in your family). It will help you keep a proper perspective when you doubt that you are a "good" parent, and it will lessen the stings that come from others who aren't in your shoes.

Ages and Stages

"All children are unique—some are just 'uniquer,'" a mom said.

Typical Child (TC):

- Infants around nine months develop early intentional communication by way of shared attention, vocalization, and gesture. This is very important for communicative development and interpersonal connections.

- Infants (as early as ten months) show awareness and interest in other children who are crying. When another baby cries, the infant looks toward the sounds and the baby itself.

> "The fundamental job of a toddler is to rule the universe."
>
> —Unknown

> Some Humor. A few of the Ten Toddler Rules: If I like it, it's mine. If it's in my hand, it's mine. If I can take it from you, it's mine. And finally, if it's broken, it's yours.

- By eighteen months of age, children will attempt to comfort a crying person by patting them or sharing a toy with them.
- Around two years of age, children begin to use emotion words, such as "happy" and "sad," and desire words, such as "want" and "need."
- By three years of age, children are able to attribute their own feelings and motives to others. For example, they may say that mommy is sad when they feel sad themselves. They begin to use words and understand concepts, such as "know, think, and pretend." When they start preschool, most children have a good understanding of others' emotions, even if they can't act upon this knowledge appropriately.

Spectrum Child (SC):

Ask for testing to be done by a pediatrician if you notice these signs. Early intervention is crucial.

- An infant displays a lack of eye contact, smiling, and auditory attention to speech.
- By twelve months, a child doesn't interact with its parents or have "meaningful gestures," such as waving to greet someone or pointing to an object to get an adult's attention. If someone wants the child to pay attention to an object, the child seems to not hear them.
- Texture aversions (how something feels to a child) is one of the first signs that appear. Food aversions are also

common, and feeding therapy may be needed with the help of an occupational therapist or speech-language therapist.

- A child experiences meltdowns when transitioning from what he or she wants to do (his or her world).

Since impaired communication is a touchstone on the spectrum, here's some information from Christina L. Rigney, MS, CCC-SLP, a speech pathologist:

Many children land in the early intervention program in the schools FIRST. They are labeled as "speech and language delayed," given a federal code (that describes the child's disability), and/or a "wait-see" approach is taken. Then later—if they don't progress, to the family's satisfaction or expectation—the families seek additional assessments (due to their observations of lack of progress), which is usually from a private practitioner of some kind.

If the practitioner suspects a spectrum disorder, the child should ideally be referred to a neuropsychiatrist to get a confirming diagnosis and to rule out other possible causes for their presented behaviors and lack of development. Families should then pursue both educationally based, and private practice speech language pathology services to assist their child and family with communication difficulties.

The verbal children sometimes get labeled as Oppositional Defiance Disorder (ODD) early on, but more often they are placed in speech pathology or early intervention.

> "The earlier you get treatment the better."
>
> —Clinical social worker

This is primarily a disorder of language, and affects the way language is understood, interpreted, and used. Because we are humans, we never cease communicating even when we think we are not. For some of these families, this becomes a pervasive difficulty for every exchange no matter how formal or informal the setting.

Joint Attention

Joint attention is the shared reference of an object between caregiver and child. This is the process of early socialization by way of circular reactions, which are goal-directed behaviors used to "connect" in some way to another person. It emerges over time based on sensory experiences, motor control, and cognition. ASD kids have varying degrees of joint attention, but for many the lack of it is an early sign that there is something wrong with their ability to connect and relate to people around them.

> Empathy is identification with another's feelings, either directly or vicariously.

Around eighteen months, children start with imitative play— rudimentary at first, but later playing "house" or imagining that a toy figure is a racecar driver. By this point, kids can see that people have distinct roles and behaviors. But it's not until around a child's fourth birthday that he really grasps the fact he and others, even Mom and Dad, have separate thoughts and feelings.

Preschool through Kindergarten

The Basics

What are the basics we learn as preschoolers? We learn to share, take turns, and trade toys—and we never outgrow the need to master these skills. How do you feel when someone at work refuses to share information you need, or won't trade weekends with you when you need to be off? And how do you feel when another driver speeds up through the intersection when it is your turn to go? As adults, we call those people selfish, controlling, and egotistical. When you learn and apply the "pre-school" skills in your daily life, things go much smoother.

> The best present is *to be present*. Stop and share your presence with your child.

If you're a spectrum child/adult, these social skills don't come easy. They don't make sense to you, but they are needed in the everyday lives of children and adults.

"Sam doesn't share with anyone. I guess he thinks he'll lose control," a mom said. So how do you help your child on the spectrum share? Help him learn another's perspective.

- Set the scene. Identify a "friend" for your child (this can be a typical child or a spectrum child). Talk to his or her mother, explaining your situation and challenges. "Will you help me help my child?" Tell her what you need and your plan—a play date—for the four of you.
- When the play date occurs, which may work best in your home, include lots of praising for both children whenever they successfully share and take turns. Both children will love the attention from adults. Their emotional tanks will be filled and they'll be encouraged to keep sharing and taking turns. The other mom will learn skills and experience your world, one that she may not have known before.
- Move slowly to the sidelines as play progresses in the right direction.

- If you don't have the time for a playday, engage someone you trust to "play" with your child. You can teach others to take each step with the children in this activity.

Theory of Mind

Theory of mind is the development of intellect, ideas, imagination, reason, and understanding of the world that changes over time with new experiences. Theory of mind continues to develop throughout life's span. Think of the way you thought you knew so much as a teen and how much more you know about the world and people *now*.

Theory of mind can be so limited for an SC. The negative side is obvious—they may not understand and become upset if someone doesn't know the answer to their question, and they may have trouble anticipating what others will say or do in a variety of situations. This results in difficulty understanding that others have thoughts and emotions, and it can make the spectrum person appear self-centered, eccentric, or uncaring.

The positive side is that many SCs have difficulties lying. Some individuals on the spectrum may believe that others always know what they are thinking. While not pleasant for teachers or parents, the beginning of telling lies by a child can be positive, in that it is a developmental milestone—one that then needs to be addressed as something that is negative.

Some parents say, "My spectrum child knows how to lie, that's for sure—but I'm not sure he understands the consequences." So, how do you work with these issues? Let's talk about "social stories." These help individuals "read" and understand social situations and respond with appropriate behaviors. It was developed by Carol Gray and seeks to provide answers to questions that autistic persons may need to know to interact appropriately with others (for example, the answers to who, what, when, where, and why in social situations). The use of social stories can motivate children to question why others see the world in different ways (see Glossary).

Kate's Good Day
(Age four, one year after diagnosis.)

Today was a good day for Kate. Let me count the ways.

1. Gym class: There were twice as many kids as usual (make-ups). Several of the kids were disruptive and distracting. Kate focused on the teacher and the task for the whole class time.

2. Birthday party: Kate's friend, Declan, had his fourth birthday at Pixieland today. (Pixieland is an amusement park geared for six-and-under kids.) Kate was able to stay for the entire two hours; she was able to sit through not one, but TWO loud renditions of the "Happy Birthday" song, and we had no meltdowns.

3. Swinging: Kate has been practicing swinging for awhile now—trying to pump. Today, she mastered it, and spent nearly two hours of total bliss swinging all by herself. She was very proud.

4. Eating: Kate asked for a cheeseburger and celery for dinner. She ate neither, but was very insistent that she wanted them—two things she's never, ever asked for in her life. Almost always the answer to "What do you want for dinner?" is "Spaghetti." (Extreme food preferences and aversions are normal for autistic children.)

5. Relating: At one point while Kate was swinging, I was sitting and staring into space. She asked, "What are you thinking, Mommy?" And then she turned it into a silly game. When Tom came home with the cheeseburger, she said, "OH!!!! You GOT it!!!" Like it was manna from heaven. While praying tonight, I said, "Thank you, God, for swinging." And Kate said, "Thank you that I go high now and can pump." Today was a very good day. Today, Kate seemed like a normal kid. Pretty wonderful.

(Elizabeth and Tom also have a nine-year-old son, Adam, who is a cancer survivor, and Kate is a seven-year-old spectrum kid, who is progressing well.)

Elementary through Middle School

Friends and "Kind of Friends"

"He's getting bigger like the typical kids his age, but is different. The same, but different," Kevin's mom said.

"Sally's adjusting to one friend now, but add even one more and she shuts down. The crowded playground can be a disaster."

Sally's emotional tank plunges to empty—fast. She has nothing to fall back on and she either screams or retreats into her own world. Either way, she doesn't relate to the other children—those unwritten social rules are rough.

> A spectrum child may interact with adults better than his peer group.

Work on asking questions at home, which is a safe place. Get her outside of herself. Tell her specifically what you mean, in a calm voice.

*"None of us are mind-readers,
especially spectrum kids."*

Bullying and Feeling Alone

"A lot of children who are on the autism spectrum just tend to take it, or they'll physically fight back. They just don't have the skills, words, or techniques—and just don't know what to do," a specialist said.

Parents feel their spectrum child's emotional (and physical) pain. "You just want to go to the playground and protect them, or scream at the staff to *do* something." There are some programs that deal with the bullying issue, and children practice role-playing exercises and rehearse statements to help improve their defenses.

"I don't really like what you did, so I want you to stop," a child says, looking into a mirror (so he can see his facial expressions to know what he looks like when he's talking).

The programs help with self-esteem, and the child can gain confidence, helping him on his journey later in life, also. (See Resource Three, Sociable Kidz.)

IEPs (Individualized Education Programs)

- Educate yourselves on your child's right to a "free and appropriate" public education. You need to learn how the system works because you'll be dealing with it throughout much of your child's academic career.
- Before your first IEP meeting, talk with other parents and anyone who is familiar with these meetings—and ask them what you need to ask for. This is probably a whole new situation for you.

- IEP meetings include anyone who is *invited* to attend. (You may also invite anyone you want to attend.) Along with you as parents (guardians), your child's teacher(s), counselor, special education specialist, paraprofessionals (teacher's aides), and others who interact with your child such as doctors, psychiatrists, psychologists, and advocates may be present. There may be speech, occupational, and physical therapists also. It depends on your child's needs and services. Some professionals outside the school may attend, or they may be on a phone call during the meeting.

- Feel free to ask very direct questions at team meetings and don't stop asking questions until your internal voices are quieted by the answers you receive.

- Goals should be child specific and not over-generalized or cut and pasted from a data bank of goals. The goals should be measurable and meaningful for your child—not too high to attain, or too low that the child has almost mastered the goal.

- You have the right to two-way communication and should receive answers from your service providers within a reasonable amount of time. Also, you can request a team meeting at any time to discuss concerns about the appropriateness and effectiveness of the interventions. Parents may invite whomever they want to attend the team.

- Remember, the IEP is designed specifically to address *academic needs* for your child, and it won't be the holistic approach necessary to deal with your child's idiosyncrasies, which need to be addressed by a private practitioner.

The IEP is for public school performance and some specialized private schools.

- Public services should not be the only services your child receives. They are useful, helpful, and necessary, but it can be a frustrating process to obtain them—no matter where your child is on the spectrum. If your child is on the mild end of the spectrum, the behavior may be even harder to diagnose—his needs may not be "needy" enough to qualify for public services—and you don't want him to fall through the cracks.

- You are at the helm of your child's academic career, and many parents feel powerless. Get help from those who've been there in the form of an advocate, if needed. Start early if you see the need for an advocate—the process is a long (involved) one. You may need someone to come alongside at times.

- If your child doesn't meet the government criteria for public services and falls through the cracks, seek help from local autism support groups.

"At school, my son Curt holds it together all day, then when he hits home—he explodes." Be prepared for the afternoon let-down. Forewarned is forearmed.

When to Hold Tight, and When to Let Go

If your child has a sprained ankle, you wrap it with an elastic bandage to give the ankle strength and support as it heals. You don't wrap it too tight—cutting off the blood supply—and you don't wrap it too loose—making it ineffectual—but just right. You can wrap an emotional bandage around your hurting child, but it isn't so easy to assess how tight or loose is this bandage. Each day (sometimes each hour), decisions need to be made to hold on tight, or to step back.

- Do I tell him he's been invited to my friend's house to play with her son?
- Can he handle it if he goes—what if he melts down?
- Should I stay there and be the go-between?

When do you loosen the grip, and when do you tighten it? You know your child better than anyone, so trust your instincts. But also, trust other's advice on your journey—get their input. They may see things more objectively than you. You need all the input you can get—two, or more, brains are better than one.

The decisions you make will depend on your own personality (see Resource One) and your background in dealing with family situations. Keep your eyes open for more clues and helpful hints for decision making.

"I wish I could get into his brain and emotions and see what he's thinking and how he's doing."

Teens through Adults

Typical teens deal with hormones, driving, dating, and dances. They may be tempted with drugs, so keeping an open communication line with them is important. Sometimes depression can creep in when they compare themselves to their peers. As they mature, they distance themselves from their parents to establish their individuality. That's typical for teens—keep reminding yourself that "this too shall pass."

Now, spectrum teens experience those dilemmas and have spectrum challenges on top. Talk to them about the "regular" issues, and the added challenges in a safe place, in a calm voice, and let them express their feelings. Their emotions may swing from bitterness, withdrawal, and depression to arrogance, thinking, *I'm way smarter than those regular kids.* Their emotions are real to them and they need a safe and secure person with which to interact. It's not easy for you the parent, but it's necessary for your child.

Sometimes spectrum children can't identify their emotions, another hallmark of spectrum disorders, and they need help with signature words for feelings. Encourage your child/teen to be involved in youth activities, Special Olympics, or whatever their talent or interest—just support them along the way.

Spiritual

Because of this demanding journey, parents may only focus on the emotional, mental, and physical parts of the child. Don't neglect the part you can't see—the spiritual. Encourage her to attend church with you and be with other children. Simply talking to God with your child each day connects your child to Him. Your child learns to walk, talk, and

> Four-year-old Kate's prayer: "I want to give everyone God."

become a person by being with you. Much of his learning is caught, not taught. That's true of his spiritual journey, also. Your life is the lesson he's learning.

A Year on the Floor
Mary's journey with her granddaughter, Jenny:

My granddaughter Jenny was born in 1988. She was an unusually beautiful baby with dark brown eyes and hair so dark it seemed almost black in the sunlight. She hit all the "marks" as an infant and toddler. At fourteen months old, our life with Jenny was hurled into a dark tunnel—eye contact stopped, words stopped—her world consisted of herself, specific well-loved toys, and her routine.

As her primary caregiver, I chose to spend a year on the floor with my precious granddaughter to enter her world, or bring her into mine. She was four years of age at that time and I was beginning to think I would lose her forever if steps were not taken to seduce her into our world.

One of the most significant moments in my memory happened during her birthday party. We had cake, hats, gifts . . . all the trimmings to make it a special day for Jenny. The Pooh Bear characters were grabbed off the cake and carried in her sticky little hands from then on.

As I sat on the floor with Jenny playing with a toy, she turned it upside down to allow the pieces to fall and began using the base as another hammer to pound with. Then, without looking up, she touched my arm in a very gentle way. What a gentle touch. It felt warm and sweet as the tiny hand lay on my arm for a split second, and then slid off, leaving a feeling of warmth that went straight to my heart. She had never done anything like that before. All afternoon I felt that warm, gentle touch. What joy lay in that simple touch. How it lingered with me for such a long time.

Then it occurred to me. The touch! The autistic touch was like no other. It was almost magical, unlike anything I had experienced. Was that gesture from Jenny saying, "Touch me. I need your touch?" or was that divine intervention, saying, "Even though she doesn't seem to want it, Jenny needs your loving, tender touch." I don't know, but it was then that things began to change between Jenny and me. I took every opportunity to touch her. Oh, I had picked her up, hugged her limp body, kissed her every morning, but it was different. I learned to allow my fingertips to slide down her arm, watching her eyes light up at the sensation of it. I, too, could feel it register in my own heart. There were times when we would be sitting together on the floor and I would caress her tiny toes. When I would stop she would move her toes closer to me.

Finally, she wanted something.

Mary titled her website, *The Autistic Touch*, because it was through touch that she and Jenny really began to connect. It was much later before Jenny was comfortable enough to show her affection, but she really needed the natural love that is so simple—she needed to bond, somehow, with someone.

The following is known as the Serenity Prayer. It is accredited to Reinhold Neibuhr, but it may have been passed down through the ages before being recorded:

> Prayer: Help me each day, in each decision, and give me the trust to leave it in your hands, Lord.

God grant me the SERENITY to
accept the things I cannot change;
COURAGE to change the things I can;
and WISDOM to know the difference.
Living one day at a time;
enjoying one moment at a time;
accepting hardships as the pathway to peace.
Taking, as He did, this sinful world
as it is, not as I would have it.
Trusting that He will make all things
right if I surrender to His Will;
that I may be reasonably happy in this life
and supremely happy with Him forever in the next.

Amen

Letters floating in your spoon:

P - E - A - C - E - F - U - L

He leads me beside peaceful streams.

—Psalm 23:2b NTL

Chapter Four

Making Sense of Your Child's Senses

Let us not become weary in doing good, for at the proper time we will reap a harvest if we do not give up.

—Galatians 6:9

Are you weary of trying to stay one step ahead when dealing with your child's *senses*?

"The things he does just doesn't make sense," a mom said. They may not make sense to her or the rest of the world, but they make sense to her child, and they are probably the only ways he knows to interact.

The Basic Five Senses

The basic five senses may be experienced this way through your child's altered filter:

- **See.** "The light outside hurts my eyes. I need stronger sunglasses." And you thought it was just fluorescent light *inside* that freaked him out. To some children, certain colors are offensive, and he or she will only eat foods that are a certain color.
- **Hear.** "Those people are too loud." Those people are quietly talking—on the other side of the room. Noise sensitivity means a fear of alarms, sirens, vacuum cleaners, or firecrackers—and your child will scream at the top of her lungs when loud noises occur. (She is trying to drown out the noise and have some control.) Also, she can hear your whispers from another room, or says she can hear the humming of wires in the walls.

- **Taste**. He gags and spits out the very small spoonful of ice cream that you finally got him to try. Everyone loves ice cream don't they? Also, new research suggests that we have taste receptors in the back of the naso-pharynx—so we can taste smells. These children can gag on appearances, consistencies, and temperature of food, also.

- **Smell**. You've searched and researched non-smelling-of-any-kind washing products to please your child, and you've not been successful—no matter what the label says or promises. Also, anything can set off a child. They become distracted, overstimulated, unable to ignore the smell, gag, or not ever seem to adjust to the smell—and some children say certain smells are "loud."

- **Touch**. Items are too scratchy, too silky, too rough, too slimy, too—too *anything*. On the other hand, it satisfies his sensory craving when he squeezes rubber balls, squishes beans in a bag, or splashes water (anywhere—even in white porcelain "bowl" in the bathroom). But later, he melts down when a spot of water appears on his clothes. You may need to spend time preparing your child for a trip to the beach (especially if you're going to be there awhile). Beware, sand!

Senses (Beyond the Five Basics)

- **Sense of order**. A place for everything and everything in its place. This sounds good and works for typical people. It especially helps those who are right brained and disorganized. However, with spectrum kids it can be carried to the extreme and become a problem. It's a place for everything (the SC's decision), and everything *always* in its place—no matter what. No moving of objects, changing of time tables, or going with the flow. He tries to control the flow to maintain his internal balance.

- **Sense of right and wrong**. Your child insists you push the shopping cart back where it belongs when you're finished loading the bags into your car—always. Your child insists you go in the "entry" door and out the "exit." Always.
- **Sense of truth**. "He always tells the truth." That's a great thing, but it comes with a price. The price consists of the people he leaves in his wake when he states facts: "You look fat today." "I don't like this food." "I don't want to ride with you because you have a funny smell." Truthful but not tactful.
- **Sense of literal**. "No, it's not really raining cats and dogs."
- **Sense of routines**. Your child wants to do certain things at certain times in certain ways. Always.
- **Sense of "correct" clothes**. "When Jenny was five, she would only wear her flannel red-and-white-checked dress. If I'd try to put anything else on her, she'd go into a complete meltdown. So, I had an idea. I sewed five identical flannel red-and-white-checked dresses. Each day she thought it was her favorite dress, and there wasn't a problem—just a happy little girl. It was a while before she realized it was more than one dress, but by that time, she was okay with it—because it *looked* like the favorite." Your child may not want the same outfit per se, but may want all his outfits to *look* and *feel* the same.
- **Sensory gross-motor stimulation**. This seeks to "wake up" his senses. Rocking back and forth as a baby teaches him to rock himself when he is older to reduce the stress

he feels. Other movements include jumping up and down, spinning, clapping his hands, and pushing and pulling objects (especially heavy objects). With all the rocking, jumping, and spinning, he may still fear heights.

Treatment and Therapy

- If your child is diagnosed with a Sensory Processing Disorder (SPD), you'll probably be connected with an occupational therapist who will use planned activities to help your child process sensory input.
- For infants, use toys with different textures. Books and toys that have rough, smooth, bumpy, and crinkly parts are also great to use. If your infant has sleep difficulty, use sound machines or white noise.
- For an older infant, a weighted blanket or a vibrating bouncy seat or crib may help.
- Movement may be a struggle for some infants, whether they crave it or are frightened by it. Rocking, bouncing, and swinging are all activities that can be introduced gradually to help them overcome their problems with movement. Infants with a need for oral input may enjoy oral massagers or vibrating toothbrushes.

Sensory Processing Disorder

For all babies, infant massage has many benefits, and even more so for those who have sensory input problems.

"Our baby is so fussy. We don't know if he's overwhelmed by sounds, or my milk doesn't agree with him, or he needs more attention and bouncing, or what. All I know is, we're exhausted. And I know more sleep would help him—and us."

"Why is our baby so startled when her siblings come chasing each other through our house? I tell them to quiet down, and even when they do, and it isn't really noisy, the baby continues to scream. I just wish she was old enough to tell us what she's feeling."

"The sweet nursery worker at our church said her arms were like Jell-O after she carried and jiggled our Brad all morning as he arched his back and screamed. Thank goodness she smiled, and looked forward to seeing him again next week. What an angel."

"I've taken Darion in for ear infections or colic, and it didn't seem to be either. Now, I'll blame his extreme fussiness on teething," a mom said. "The doctor told me to keep track over a period of time, and see if these symptoms appear repeatedly after a certain stimulus. Everything seems to be a 'stimulus' right now."

Some of the more common symptoms of SPD in infants include crying or arching their backs when being held, crying during diaper changes and baths, preferring some people over others because of volume or tone of voice, preferring not to have clothing on, and crying in a crowded place or when many people are around.

"We're not sure if our daughter will ever wear clothes. She loves running around naked, and we're so used to it, we have to catch her when she strips in the yard," a dad said—with a weary smile.

Hyposensitive versus Hypersensitive

Children with SPD can react in one of two ways to sensory information: hyposensitively or hypersensitively. When a child with SPD is hyposensitive to stimuli, they do not have as strong physical sensations as many people do. In older children, this may mean they will run into things or hurt themselves and not complain about it because this input, while painful to other people, actually feels good to them. An infant with SPD may bang his head on the floor or crib, need constant oral stimuli, such as a pacifier, or need constant movement, such as swinging or bouncing. A child with SPD who is hypersensitive will react in the opposite way. Sounds that do not sound loud to the rest of the world are deafening to them, and lights may bother their eyes when nobody else is bothered by them.

"The child's reaction can also be mixed, having qualities of both dependent on the stimuli and mode of transfer to the child's sensory system."

SPD and Other Conditions: Coexists

As children grow older, sometimes other conditions coexist with SPD. Children who struggle with ADHD also often have sensory problems. The connection between these conditions and SPD is not clear. It does not appear that one causes the other, only that they can coexist. Parents of infants with SPD should be aware of these other conditions so, as the baby grows up, parents can educate themselves about and be aware of other possible conditions.

Again, SPD means too much or too little. Just ask the three bears.

Super-sensitive-sensed Goldilocks and the Three Bears

Once upon a time, there were three bears . . . you know the story. They left their cottage and went for a walk in the woods while their soup cooled. While they were gone, in came a golden-haired girl with super-sensitive-sense issues.

Because she was tired from her walk, she tried to climb on the papa bear's chair—but it was too high. Then she tried the momma's, but it was too low. Finally, she sat in the baby bear's chair, and it was just right. Unfortunately, it broke and she landed on the floor. After she got up, she saw the bowls of soup on the table. *Ah, soup.*

She tasted the papa bear's soup, but it was too hot. Then she tried the momma bear's soup, and it was too cold. Next she tasted the baby bear's soup, and it was just right—and she ate it all up.

Being full, she grew sleepy and went upstairs for a nap. She climbed onto papa bear's bed, and it was too hard. Then she tried momma's, which was too soft. At last she tried baby bear's bed, and it was just right—and she fell asleep.

The three bears came home and saw the mess in the kitchen, with the baby's chair broken and his soup eaten. They climbed the stairs to check out the rest of the cottage and discovered the golden-haired girl fast asleep in the baby bear's bed. They exclaimed, "There she is!" The girl woke up, ran down the stairs and out of the cottage—leaving the mess for momma bear to clean up.

You may have a super-sensitive-sense child in your house, but your "too high—too low—too hot—too cold—too hard—too soft" child doesn't balk on purpose to frustrate you. That's how she's wired. And whether your child is golden-haired or brown-haired, she or he needs your understanding and a bed that "fits." Just be thankful that she finally sat in a chair, ate some soup, and slept for a while.

A Different Country (or Planet)

Typical adults have sensory filters that literally filter out non-meaningful stimuli.

But what if you were in a strange country where you didn't know the language, or the customs, and you were bombarded with high-pitched sounds, flashing strobe lights, and everyone knew what to do—except you? And just when you began to understand a few words or actions, everyone decided to change their words and their actions. When these people approached you, you didn't know if they'd hug you or punch you. Nothing at all made sense. Welcome to the land of broken sensory filters.

"So that's why my parenting skills don't work. I need a new parenting manual for my spectrum child who is trying to figure out our 'country,'" a parent exclaimed. This book is written to share the new parenting skills you will need as you enter your child's "country," and as you bring him into yours. You may have to remind yourself daily, hourly, moment by moment, that your "country" doesn't make sense to him, and he's not doing strange things to you on purpose to overwhelm you. Carve out the time to pray about each challenging broken sensory filter.

Making Sense (for Yourself and Others) of His Senses
By Tim Tucker

When they ask, "How do you keep up with everything?"
show them pictures of him smiling with his therapists and teachers,
show them everything he could not do three months ago, and say,
"Like this."

When they ask, "How does all this sensory stuff work?"
take their hands and stroke a purring kitten,
wrap them in an embrace, dance with a symphony,
bring them out into the sun and let it warm their faces, and say,
"Like this."

When they ask, "How does your son being different affect your life?"
draw them a picture of a large dairy farm with endless herds
and one remarkable, dancing, purple, polka-dotted cow
whom everyone marvels and smiles at, and say,
"Like this."

When they ask, "How do you make sense of his need for order?"
point to the heavens and the procession of constellations

and the orbiting planets and the traveling moon, and say,
"Like this."

When they ask, "How can repeating the same thing over and over
help him?"
show them the waves as they roll on to the shore,
recede back to the great ocean, and then return once more;
show them the rain falling to nourish the fields, and the water rising back
up to the sky, and say,
"Like this."

When they ask, "How does he communicate with pictures?"
show them the trees and the sky and the lilies of the field,
bring out photos of the Pieta, distant galaxies, and the helices of DNA,
and say,
"Like this."

When they ask, "How does it feel to speak to someone all day every day
and have him never really talk back?"
Face the open air, kneel, and pray, and say,
"Like this."

When they ask, "How will you deal with the future?"
show them the depth of his great blue eyes,
hum his favorite song and let them see his head fall to your shoulder,
and kiss him gently on his cheek, and say,
"Like this."

And when they ask, "How do you parent a child with autism?"
Stand with your arms open, your chest out, and your head high, and say,
"Like this."

❧

We aren't perfect parents; no one is. But God wants us to be faithful parents. We can do that with his help, "for your Father knows what you need before you ask him" (Matt. 6:8b).

Letters floating in your spoon:

R-E-N-E-W-S

He renews my strength.

—Psalm 23:3a NLT

Chapter Five

Transitions, Tantrums, Stickers, and Stims

Circumstances may appear to wreck our lives and God's plans, but God is not helpless among the ruins.

—Eric Lindell, Olympian and missionary

Josh's screams reverberated off the metal ceiling in the grocerystore, and echoed from aisle to aisle. Janet dropped to her knees and huddled over her sobbing son, promising him everything she could afford to buy. Nothing worked. Shopping carts maneuvered around the corners of Janet's aisle, as shoppers peered at the "scene" unfolding. When Janet gave up wrestling Josh, she attempted to drag him out the door. She left *another* cart of groceries in the aisle. "My life's a wreck . . ."

Meltdowns and Stickers

The grocery shoppers (and clerks) assumed this child was just undisciplined, and he wanted something his mother wouldn't buy. They'd never suspect the real reason for the meltdown. They wouldn't guess that this wasn't just a "shopping" fit, but the control issues happen at home also—even first thing in the morning for many families.

Here's a typical morning at Janet's house, in her words:

Suffering throughout the Bible: "As an example of patience in the face of suffering, take the prophets who spoke in the name of the Lord."

—James 5:10

7:15 a.m.: "What a great morning!" Josh yelled as he burst into the kitchen, pounced on his chair, knelt on one knee, and started swinging his other leg. For a change, he had slept well and faced the day with unexpected (from his norm) enthusiasm. I was running late and had just realized, *No more Frosted Flakes in the pantry!*

I put out three other kinds of cereal, smiled, and said in a calm voice, "You get to choose which one you want today."

Josh's eyes narrowed as he yelled, "I hate those! Where's my Frosted Flakes?"

"We're out of them." I saw his shoulders hunch and decided to try one more time. "I'm going to the store today and I'll get more."

"I hate those cereals!" Josh screamed, and he ran out of the room.

7:20 a.m.: *And good morning to you, too.*

"But those who hope in the LORD will renew their strength. They will soar on wings like eagles; they will run and not grow weary, they will walk and not be faint."

—Isaiah 40:31

Now, I just needed to get him to eat anything, make sure he had on all his clothes (the same kind he wore every day, but make sure they are clean), and get him to the car, into the car, out of the car, into the school, down the hall, into his schoolroom—and warn his teacher about the storm brewing.

I was exhausted as I dragged myself out to the car. *Is it ever going to get easier?*

Yes, I know all children are unique—but mine seems "uniquer."

Stickers (or Whatever Else Works)

Your child reacts and looks forward to the promise of a sticker (or whatever works for your child) and the reward or prize that follows. You may hear these words from your sticker-seeking child.

"I get a sticker for that."

"Do I get a sticker for that?"

"That deserves five stickers."

Suggestions to help? See "Applied Behavior Analysis (ABA)" and other helps listed in the Glossary. Parents of children on the spectrum don't take success stories for granted. Ultimately, every child has their own success—some more dramatic than others—but every milestone is important. Since ABA is expensive, here are some basic behavior modification suggestions to use: good, consistent expectations and discipline; involve a strong league of specialists; reinforcing good behavior; and taking away a desired object or "want" if behavior is negative.

> "It is not giving children more that spoils them; it is giving them more to avoid confrontation."
>
> —John Gray

What's a "sticker" for *you* as a parent? An uninterrupted afternoon nap? An entire day without a call from your child's school? And there are some days you deserve five stickers. When you're running on empty emotionally, look at Chapter Eight, Caring for the Caregiver, for suggestions for filling that tank.

Meltdowns verses Temper Tantrums

A meltdown is the result of some sort of overwhelming stimulation—usually a mystery to parents and other adults as to the cause. It can come suddenly and catch everyone by surprise. However, a good therapist can help by giving you the "ABC" approach:

A: Antecedent (what happened directly before the meltdown)

B: Behavior (what type of reaction the child had)

C: Consequence (what happened next)

Your child can be mapped so you can discover his pattern. After a meltdown, these children need to withdraw and slowly collect themselves at their own pace. However, with a temper tantrum, the child is looking for attention and demanding their way—consciously manipulating the people around him. He knows what he's doing and has learned what "works" to get what he wants.

Some professionals think a spectrum child manipulates by meltdowns; however, many think they are simply overwhelmed by sensory stimulation and don't understand what others are thinking, or how to communicate their frustration. Meltdowns can be brought on by a change in routine, a sugar crash, an impending virus, and/or an irrational or developmental fear.

Some adults who've had no discipline in their lives have more trouble fitting into society—whether they have special needs or not. Examine your parenting style and the grandparents' parenting style. Does mom try to keep peace at any price and keep the family "running smoothly"? This is a good thing, but over time it can develop into spoiling—and she doesn't even realize it.

"Tyrone's never been told 'NO' and I try to cut him some slack—but I'm not sure what is a neurological situation, and what's just being spoiled." Ask professionals and others on your journey for guidelines and suggestions. A professional gave these guidelines for parents: if the actions violate any of the following situations, then they must be altered, eliminated, or mediated.

- Good health
- Healthy family relations
- Balanced attentions
- Community safety

Often parents and kids just need a few signs, gestures, or rehearsed phrases to use during situations—a script, so to speak. Plan ahead with your unique "script."

Different Results

You have to realize that typical children (TCs) and spectrum children (SCs) both get frustrated, tired, angry, and may have meltdowns. However "time outs" and discipline provide very different results.

Typical Children	Spectrum Children
TCs will eventually obey.	SCs won't obey as soon.
TCs can apply new skills.	SCs usually can't apply skills to new situations—they must be taught over and over and over in each new situation where the behavior applies.
TCs will learn from the discipline and act differently in the future.	SCs don't learn or act differently in the future without more intervention—they need to learn to use skills in the new situations.
	Over time, and with lots of follow through with behavior modification, SCs' actions may change, so don't give up. The more behavior modification is done consistently, the more peaceful your life will become. Keep on keeping on.

Typical Children	Spectrum Children
TCs' parents think parenting is difficult at times. They may say to Brandon's (SC) parents, "We know how you feel. Our Johnny is so strong willed too."	SCs' parents *know* parenting is difficult *most* of the time—and they don't even answer Johnny's parents' statement. They just smile wanly—and probably feel isolated, angry, and resentful of the *petty* problems others talk about.

Transition to New Event

Summer Fun—Plan Ahead!

You're taking your family to the beach. Bathing suits packed, sunscreen packed, new place, lots of new people, and it's the Fourth of July weekend! For some children (and adults) this holiday scenario, as well as many other common summertime activities, represents an overwhelming experience and may actually be a painful event for them.

Instead of a fun-filled weekend, those who over-respond to sensory stimuli might have this experience instead: Scratchy bathing suit and itchy sand. Many people surround and accidentally bump him—he bumps back on purpose. Now comes the evening, exhaustion sets in from trying to "keep it together" all day—and then, the loud fireworks display. That's the final blow to his senses and an inconsolable meltdown erupts.

Your child's nervous system receives input from the five senses and then forms an inappropriate response—a meltdown, crying, physical aggression, "tuning out" of the situation, or increased inappropriate stimming.

Plan ahead—especially for "summer fun" and other special outings and holiday adventures. This may need to be repeated over and over—and over.

- Prepare a "social story" to review with your child before attending a new event or activity. Have him "read" it to you.

  > Glossary Helps: Social Story

- Make sure your child is well rested and not hungry before the event. (Take extra snacks that he likes.)
- If in a very stimulating environment, make sure you take frequent breaks away in a quiet place, if possible.
- Use a pair of noise-reducing headphones, or whatever works for your child.
- Have items ready in case of a meltdown. Find a quieter place where you can run with your child. Hug your child tightly (deep pressure). Have crunchy food or a chew toy for him to relieve stress.
- Seek the help of your pediatrician and a qualified occupational therapist trained in sensory integration.

Transitional Objects

These are designated objects that a child *must* carry from one location or event to another (hopefully, they are even remotely connected to the location or event). They distract the child from stimming, and help the difficulties of the transition by giving her a "responsibility" and distraction.

> Amusement parks may not be amusing —get a special pass to stand in the front of lines, carry your "emergency kit," and plan for breaks from all the "amusement."

It helps so much if the object is small and can be hidden in her pocket or purse. During school, if touching the object is necessary, let the teacher know beforehand so that it can be done discreetly and out of sight of other children.

Stims

Have you ever tapped your pencil, bitten your nails, twirled your hair, or paced? Have you ever jiggled your leg until someone said, "You're shaking the car!" Then, you've engaged in stimming.

The term "stimming" is short for self-stimulatory behavior, and it is used to manage anxiety, fear, anger, and other negative emotions. In a person on the spectrum, stimming usually refers to specific behaviors such as flapping, rocking, spinning, or repeating words and phrases.

What's the difference between typical stimming and spectrum stimming? The *choice* of the stim—what is acceptable in our society, jiggling your leg or flapping your fingers? Also, the *quantity* of the stim—occasional leg jiggling verses constant finger flapping. People on the spectrum stim to help manage anxiety, fear, anger, and other negative emotions, but it also helps them handle overwhelming sensory input (too much noise, light, heat, etc.). The constant stimming can hinder their interaction with others, especially in typical situations (school, playing, even family functions). A child who regularly needs to pace the floor or slap himself in the head certainly sets himself apart from typical students, friends, and others who don't understand the different behavior.

At times, stimming helps manage challenging situations, but when it becomes a major distraction or causes physical harm to self or others, it needs to be modified. That can be tricky, but several approaches may be helpful. Applied Behavioral Analysis and Occupational Therapy can be helpful. Here, you are a team member with the professionals, and together you can make decisions about how much stimming to allow, and where. Saving "major" (whatever that means for you and your child) stimming for times at home may also help.

~❧

Letters floating in your spoon:
G - U - I - D - E - S

He guides me along right paths, brining honor to his name.

—Psalm 23:3b NLT

Chapter Six

Doctors, Dentists, and Hair Cuts . . . Oh My!

God writes across some of our days,
"Will explain later."

—Vance Havner

First things first. Be sure the doctor, dentist, or barber/hairstylist will be comfortable with your child. A talk on the phone with the office will make these transitions more pleasant for your child, you, and the people on the other end of the phone. Be honest and tell them what behaviors your child exhibits and that you want the best situation for everyone. Make sure they are comfortable, and you are too. Read the rest of this chapter and see if other parents' suggestions might work for you.

What do ASD children want (need)? They want situations that are familiar, structured, known, and situations that they expect. Where is that not going to happen? The doctor's and the dentist's offices. When you put an "un" in front of the things ASD children want/need, they become triggers. Depending on the issues and age of your child, he needs to have you by his side.

> Specialists such as ENT's (Ear, Nose, Throat) may give extra "helps" to consider for your child's visit.

Possible Triggers

- **The unexpected.** Fear of what's going to happen—changes to schedules, routines, anything. Also, he may fear what he's already experienced. It is the *expected*—but if he didn't like it before, he probably won't like it now.

- 🐾 **The unknown.** What's the stranger going to do? Touch the child, stick stuff in his mouth, what?
- 🐾 **The unstructured.** How long does he have to sit here (waiting room/consultation room)? He is surrounded by new people, new smells, new everything.
- 🐾 **The unfamiliarity.** What's this stuff (equipment)?

Visit to the Doctor

> Always have your "emergency kit" with you. The items may change depending on the age and needs of your child. Have items for you, too!

Don't walk out your door before you grab your child's "emergency kit." This can be a tote filled with her special drinks, foods, games, chewing "toys," transition cards, Band-Aids, a change of clothes, whatever you've ever used or think you will ever need in an "emergency."

Next, add your "emergency" items. Wipes, cell phone, meds you may need, your plan book for the day, anything you've ever needed or think you might need again in an "emergency."

Sensory Difficulties

Lights. Strip fluorescent lighting can be experienced as painful and distracting. Even the use of pen lights can trigger reactions in some children.

Touch. "Now, jump up on the table," says the nurse. Your child refuses. He's probably thinking, "What's the white paper for?"

"Take off your clothes," the nurse continues (as if he's going to do that). That's easy for a typical child, but it took you two hours to get him to put *on* clothes this morning—much less take them off now. And mom thinks: *How am I going to get his clothes off without a meltdown? That'll short circuit our visit for sure. I'm so exhausted getting here—not sure if I can finish this visit.*

"Open your mouth." His mouth locks tighter as he wonders, "Why?"

Autism is primarily a disorder of language and communication—and this is the primary hallmark that hangs an "alphabet" on them, or releases them from the label. Language processing interferes with reception and expression. Children on the spectrum need to be talked to *differently*, taught *differently*, and given commands *differently*.

Spectrum children can be hyposensitive to touch, meaning that they don't feel pain even when examined, and they don't react because they can't decode the pain.

"Terrance runs full speed, hits the wall and bounces off—falls on the floor—gets up, shakes his head—and keeps running," one mom says. "We're living in the ER with sprains and bruises, but he never complains so I'm not sure when he's hurt. It's so frustrating, and I don't want him to be neglected. Also, the nurses are beginning to look at me funny."

"Bobby has the weirdest responses to pain. He laughs, hums, or just makes funny sounds. When he does that at different times, we have to check and be sure he isn't hurt."

Spectrum children can also be hypersensitive to touch, meaning that the slightest touch appears to be painful. They pull away when being examined, and the instruments used (to listen to their chests, look in their ears, and down their throats) seem to cause discomfort. You can develop a scale using different pictures/facial expressions/colors indicating the severity of pain next to each number. Body charts (pointing to the *part* of the body that hurts) can also help your child communicate their pain.

Noise. Take one waiting room filled with crying babies; add a TV cartoon show blaring and/or music playing; and then add nurses calling patients' names, parents calling their children's names, and you have a disaster waiting to happen—a cocktail of sensory bombardment.

Personal Space and Body Perception. Many waiting rooms are packed with patients and parents—all of them too close for your child's comfort level. He needs more personal space. No one knows that, but when he starts acting out, all they see is a child throwing a tantrum "for no reason."

Gratefully, your child's name is called, and you go the examination room. However, the nurse and doctor come even closer to your child than the people in the waiting room, and they want to touch his body. Personal space is gone, and if he is non-verbal, he can't even tell them where it hurts—if he does hurt. You want to explain that he struggles with body awareness.

You may be thinking, "My child is just the opposite about personal space. He's too close to everyone else's space—leans near their faces, wants to touch them." Whatever your child feels about personal space, plan ahead with ways to handle the situation.

Visit to the Dentist

Put yourself in your child's place: You don't understand why you're going to a place where a man or woman will look into your mouth with strange equipment, and you're having to lie back in a chair and not move. On top of all that, there's a bright light shining on your face and in your eyes.

Review the helpful information for the doctor's visits. Again, plan ahead. Your child needs to hear the *reasons* he needs to go to the dentist, and why he needs to floss and brush every day. (Those tasks can be included on the daily chart at home.)

Sensory Difficulties

Touch/Noise. This is probably one of the main anxiety triggers at the dentist—tactile (touch) and auditory (noise). Mouths are extremely sensitive places, and for a person with an ASD, the sensation of a cold instrument entering their mouth could be very painful. In addition, the noise of the drills and cleaning instruments could also be a problem.

Sometimes, the taste of the cleaning paste will also have an adverse effect—as well as the strange smells.

Are there other factors that cause your child distress? Because the professionals stand so close, a whiff of perfume, a moustache, or the color of their clothing may overwhelm a super-sensitive child.

You understand the reason you lean back in the dentist's chair: to help the dentist and assistants to work in your mouth. Your child may fight this "leaning back" part. His center of gravity is "off" and he wants to lean forward. This is another issue for you to discuss with your dentist and your child before you get there.

Invasion of space. The dentist is one of the few professionals who we permit to enter our personal space. Most people find this uncomfortable but understand that the dentist needs to be so close in order to examine our teeth. For individuals with an ASD, this close proximity may well be extremely distressing. One helpful distraction may be listening to an iPod or whatever works for your child as a "distracter."

Sedation. For some people, the experience of visiting the dentist is so distressing that it may be necessary to consider sedating them. If you feel this is the case, you will need to talk to your dentist and a medical professional to discuss the options. Be sure your dentist isn't just suggesting this because your child (especially a teen) is hard to handle. You want the best options for your child and all involved. That is why it's so important to get the "right" dentist who is comfortable working with special children. There are some dentists who specifically cater to individuals with special needs, and some dentists who work occasionally with patients with additional needs.

Strategies for Doctor's and Dentist's Visits

How would *you* feel if you had an upcoming medical procedure and you didn't know where it was being done, how it was being done, how long it would take, or what would be the results? Wouldn't you want as much information as possible beforehand? Even more so does your child heading to the office of a doctor or dentist.

Preparation. Call and make an appointment to visit the office days before your child's appointment so your child becomes familiar with the people, environment, and equipment. Take photos of staff, rooms, and the building to use in a booklet (see Glossary, Social Stories) you will use when talking about the upcoming event. Use these pictures as reference points. This will desensitize your child as much as possible.

Mark the appointment date with a picture on your family's calendar. Prepare ahead of time—talk about it. Your child needs the repetition of what is coming. It may help to get the first appointment of the day, or the first afternoon appointment, to avoid long waiting times and noisy (to your child) waiting rooms. You might want to book a double appointment if your child usually requires extra time. Check to see if there's a quiet area where you can go if there's the need to do so.

The information card (see Glossary) you carry can be used in the waiting room. It gives a brief explanation of what diagnosis your child has (autism, Asperger's syndrome, etc.) and can be handed out to the public. These may be useful in the waiting room if other patients and parents have difficulty understanding your child's certain behaviors.

Patient Information for Professional Support. Before your visit, contact the doctor's/dentist's office and tell them you will provide the staff with information about your child's challenges and helpful hints so they will be prepared for the visit. They will appreciate your input.

Let them know of possible triggers specific to your child. These can include particular likes/dislikes they have, behavior, and communication strategies that work. Knowing your child's interests may help the doctor or dentist form a relationship with him, and it builds trust.

Inform them of sensory issues so that the examination and equipment can be adapted accordingly (for example, replacing a paper sheet on the examination table with a cloth one). If there is something you can bring from home to make the situation easier for your child, and for the staff, please tell them. This information could be provided through a letter, email, or phone call before the appointment. Ask if they would like something in writing to keep in your child's file.

Visual Supports. It may help to provide visual supports for your child that explain the process and what may be involved during the visit. These could include sequence cards, checklists, or photos.

Time Indicators. Time indicators are helpful when waiting—gadgets with timers are good distractors when shots are given, and it shows your child that there'll be an end to the procedure.

Rewards. Everyone likes a reward. Give your child something to look forward to and help her to see an end to the experience. Reinforce with visual supports. Sometimes just the cessation of the office visit is enough reward in itself.

Comforters and Relaxation Techniques. Comforters/distracters can help with sensory issues and fear or boredom in the waiting room, and they help you as the parent to feel more in control of the situation. You probably already carry these items in your "emergency kit" whenever you are with your child in public: earplugs, books, toys, stress balls, non-toxic rubber items to chew on—these all can help relieve his stress, and your stress, also.

Relaxation techniques such as deep breathing, counting, singing favorite songs, talking about a favorite interest, or looking at favorite books/toys can help as well. Use whatever devices work best with your child—iTouch, iPad, whatever he likes and you can afford? The main thing is to be prepared.

Haircuts

Reread all the information on visits to the doctor and the dentist, and apply what works as you plan for your child's visit to get a haircut. Be sure the stylist and the shop are comfortable working with your child and understands your situation.

Girls need extra help with hairstyles. "Brooke's scalp is so tender that I have to use special oils, brushes, and combs on her—and you'd think a pony tail would suffice—but she wants to do it herself, and then she can't get all the strands pulled back. Actually, she would just as soon never brush her hair, but I know the other girls at school would probably notice."

If you are attempting haircuts at home, use the same diversion techniques we've mentioned.

Grooming may not seem important to your child, and he'd just as soon wear the same clothes, not shower, and not comb his hair or brush his teeth. This may be the preference of a typical school-aged child as well, but because an SC doesn't pick up on social cues, he doesn't realize how much it is needed. TCs (especially boys) finally understand as they hit puberty. One mom said, "Lance is finally taking showers without being told to!"

Your child's health is of utmost importance. You as the parent are in charge while he's young, but as he matures, hopefully he will assume the responsibility to make appointments for himself and then attend them. It will seem more important to him because he sees how important it is to you.

Letters floating in your spoon:
C-L-O-S-E

Even when I walk through the darkest valley,
I will not be afraid, for you are close beside me.

—Psalm 23:4a NLT

Chapter Seven

Forewarned is Forearmed (Dealing with Crises)

But the Lord stood at my side and gave me strength. . . .

—2 Timothy 4:17a

"We seem to go from one crisis to the next. Foods Paul wouldn't eat, or he wouldn't even eat anything at all. Then he tried to make friends with the little girl next door, so he patted her on the head like she was our dog. And when she didn't respond, he patted her harder. Food and friends are our crises this week."

Your family has certain patterns dealing with a crisis, and the individuals in the family do also. We'll discuss how your family might react and some helps along the way. Then, we hope to shed light on some personal patterns of thinking and offer some helpful hints.

Two Sides of a Crisis

We tend to think of "crisis" as only a negative thing, but the Chinese use two characters with two opposite meanings for crisis. One represents "danger," and the other, "opportunity" (opportunity for growth). Both are valid.

If families view a crisis totally as "danger," dysfunction sets in. Because of the severe distress, they're unable to discover and appreciate resources from *within* the family and end up fragmented. They blame family members (and anyone else involved), prohibit the sharing of feelings, deny what is happening, and stick to rigid decisions.

"We do what we've learned to do."

Families may shut out resources from *outside* the family as well—tightening the control, enhancing the "fear" of the unknown dangers—and trust in others' opinions vanishes. They tell the professionals how to work with their child based on their own knowledge (which may be counterproductive). "My dad never let me get away with behavior like that—a good spanking will take care of that attitude," a dad said. He doesn't understand why his SC has the "attitude" he displays. Parents can get stuck in what they've experienced and shut down to others' help and enlightenment.

However, when a crisis is also viewed as "opportunity," positive growth occurs and the family remains functional. They face the reality of the situation but choose not to be thrown by it. The family chooses to work together as a team, validating each person's opinion and strength that they bring to the situation. They stay open to those outside the family unit, also, and they keep communication open. This helps not only the SC but the entire family.

"Life is hard and we've learned we can do hard," a mom said.

Again, each family member is encouraged to share their feelings as they draw upon resources (strengths) already in the family and figure out how to get what is needed to make the best decisions. Earlene, a mom, said:

> We had no idea the strengths and ideas in our typical child's mind. Marilee's really quiet. When we first heard Martin's diagnosis, we hit the wall and sat and talked many nights of

that first week . . . my, what wonderful things Marilee shared. She said she felt *needed* for the first time, and we just listened to her. We've learned so much from her, and there's no telling how this will impact her life as she grows older. We might not ever have known these things about her—and she might not have expressed them. It isn't easy for any of us, but when you see those *hidden blessings*, it give you hope for the journey.

Types of Crises

A *developmental crisis* may seem huge at the time for some: a child goes to kindergarten, a son gets his driver's license, or a daughter gets married. But these are simply stages in life that many people experience. Compare these to an *acute crisis* (such as your ASD journey). An acute crisis hastens the process of change (new normal) and hurls families into changing roles, responsibilities, routines, and lifestyles.

There are three stages of an acute crisis on the ASD journey:

- Acute crisis: Diagnosis is like being dashed on the shoreline from the first unexpected wave.
- Episodal crisis: Particular events send the family temporarily into a tailspin, like a riptide that one day appears and the next day disappears.
- Chronic crisis: The everyday expected (tidal ebb and flow) stressors that accompany life with an SC.

Tom, a dad, wrote, "As I flipped through the stack of bills, it hit. I thought the regular bills were huge—but it's nothing compared to this new stack with therapies, meds, and schooling. I wish I'd appreciated how

> "My friend had a rough day on Wednesday, she said. *A rough day.* I'd welcome *a* rough day," a mom said.

easy life was." For Tom and other parents, the bills drain their already-low emotional tank. Families need a team to help with finances. Look for someone on your journey who is good with finances and budgets, and perhaps someone else who knows the resources available, or at least where to look. Others bring a new perspective and can see your situation more clearly than you at this point. You aren't alone, and there is help out there. You can only do what you can do—but you can ask for help and assistance.

> *"The hilltop hour would not be half*
> *so wonderful if there were no dark*
> *valleys to traverse."* —Helen Keller

All family members begin a "grief" process—giving up dreams of a more perfect life. Look at Resource A again for the ways we cope (or don't cope) with stress. You need all the help you can get to walk through your "grief" process of letting go of the way you envisioned life for your family, your spectrum child, and each individual.

What is a minor difficulty to you may be major to someone else. Try to walk in their shoes.

You may be surprised as you open up to each other what bothers someone the most. It may seem minor to you, but is major to someone else. As emotional tanks drain, depression can set in quickly—keep the communication lines open. "Majors" and "minors" can change over time with everyone, even hour to hour.

Family Patterns

The family is more than the sum of individual family members; it is also how individuals relate, communicate, and solve problems.

- As family members, everyone needs to be flexible and adjust when a crisis hits. Some people only have one way to react to a crisis, and if that doesn't work, they don't know what to do.
- Family members may be too close. "You *can't* be too close." Yes, you can—when individual members depend on the family unit and don't develop on their own. When they need to be away from the family and make decisions for themselves, they don't know what to do. They need skills they've developed themselves. This can happen in an ASD family, when their entire world is inside their home. They've had to "be there" for one another, and that's good—to a certain point.
- Family members may be too distant. Individuals can keep their distance from each other, appearing cold and indifferent. They don't have emotional support from their family, as everyone turns inward.
- How does your family interact, and how do individuals give and receive support from one another? Ask family members what they need, and how that can be accomplished. Support for each other is vital. It's not easy at times, but if the members understand the importance, and receive what they need, they will be more equipped to give support to others.

However your family is functioning before the crisis—whether it be too close or distant—with some work, it can change a negative outcome to a positive one. Slow down and connect with each other on this ASD journey.

Again, the family is more than the sum of individual family members—all are needed.

Family Reactions

Crises trigger disturbing (strong) emotions. Anxiety, guilt, regret, and anger catch us by surprise as they shoot to the surface. Because family reactions are complex, the following ideas empower and enable families to better deal with crises.

Rules of conduct:

Some families have a rule (spoken or unspoken) that they are not to feel angry or to share negative feelings.

"I just want to go to bed, pull the covers over my head, and not deal with all of this," a mom said.

"Don't be so negative," her husband answered.

It's okay to feel angry—your feelings are your feelings. Don't stifle them, but talk them out in a constructive way.

Building walls and bridges:

A father hears from his friends, "How are things going at home?"

"Okay."

That ends the conversation, as he stuffs his anger, frustration, and fear deeper inside. Open up to your friends, or pastor, or someone who has experienced your journey. You need the outlet more than you know.

Stop and watch:

"We need to talk," a wife says.

"We don't have time," her husband answers.

Take a look at their refrigerator door, covered with sticky notes, packed calendars, and sticker-laden charts. They don't have time, yet they have to make time, for the most important things in their life.

> Take time to recoup and regroup. Remember, this isn't a sprint, it's a marathon.

The last straw:

The camel's back is broken with the last straw. That final straw may not be a major problem; it can be as simple as lost keys. "I can't find my keys. That isn't a big deal—so why am I on the verge of tears?" It isn't the lost keys; it's the buildup of all the other straws.

If you think you can't handle one more thing, then listen to what your body is telling you—and get help. Just someone coming alongside and helping you for a few hours will make all the difference in your coping capabilities.

You'll have lots of "last straws" on your journey. Get ahead of the game. When you feel the straws building up, step back, look at your schedule, cut back where you can, ask for help, and do whatever it takes *before* the last straw hits and you crumble. Forewarned is forearmed.

Say what you mean and mean what you say:

Be honest, but kind. Speak the truth in love. Avoid manipulating to get your way. Be a person of your word—in small and big things. Keep your promises as much as you possibly can.

Committee meetings:

Schedule (write it on the calendar) family meetings as often as needed. Who is the CEO? Are new roles needed? What are new ways of sharing the responsibilities? Be sure and include siblings—they need to be on the team and appreciated.

"We're doing this together," Carlene, a mom, said. "I look at my friends' families and I envy their life, their *typical* life, but they haven't had to dig deep and pull together like we have. I think that's been a benefit for us. They probably don't see it that way and I can tell by the look on their faces they feel sorry for us sometimes, but you can't appreciate our lives unless you're a part of our family unit."

Your ASD journey may help your family learn to grow together through feelings of accomplishment.

Personal Patterns of Thinking

Let's talk about how we interpret crises and negative events as individuals. If someone learned negative reactions as a child, they can change their perspective of a half-empty glass to a half-full or even overflowing glass. Here are some examples of how we see the "glass" and what we may think about it. If you're usually a half-full or overflowing person, this short section may give you insight into the half-empty people in your life. And, if you're that half-empty person, it may give a voice to your thoughts. You may not even realize you've thought them, or how those thoughts drain your "glass" and life.

Permanent ("*I'll* always *feel this way.*")

Half-empty: Neverending problems are their fault. "I'm a failure." "This will last forever."

Half-full: "It's bad today, but it'll be better in the future. Circumstances made it bad, but it wasn't my fault."

Pervasive (*affects everything*)

Half-empty: "I'm *always* yelling at my kids. I'm a bad mother."

Half-full: Recognizes specific explanations and doesn't generalize. "I yelled at my kids today, but the repairman was here and so much was going on." Also, "I know to ask for help when I need it."

Personalize ("*It must be my fault.*")

Half-empty: They blame themselves when blame isn't warranted.

Half-full: They recognize where problems start—and they are realistic. They accept what is their fault and what isn't. They realize they do good acts, too.

Connie's Story

Connie, usually a half-full to overflowing young mom, hit a depression after her third child was born.

Everything in my life was fine, and I couldn't understand this heavy-blanket-draped-over-me feeling. I was a morning person and usually got up smiling and was ready to experience another great day. But for the past few months, I hadn't been sleeping at night (and couldn't even blame it on my baby who slept seven hours straight). I'd drag myself out of bed, and trudge through the day.

My husband, Ron, finally said, "Go the doctor—something's wrong." And sure enough—post-partum depression. My doctor suggested a short-term medication. I got some sleep, started to exercise some, and after a while my sunshiny self (as Ron calls it) returned. For the first time in my life, I had had to cope with being a different person, and I had a small inkling of people who saw their glass as half-empty.

It was during my down time that my dear half-empty-glass friend, Luwanda, said to me, "I'm sorry you're going through this, but that's what I deal with every day. I have to force myself to get up, and choose to be thankful for the day and what I have. My mom and I both can fall back into our negative talk—complaining about our husbands, how tired we are—and we both finally realized that our view of our day is a choice. We now pray, asking God to give us what we don't have on our own, and He is so faithful. The positive view and words during the day come easier as we choose to have Him change our thoughts."

Well, when she said she dealt with her half-empty viewpoint every day, that jarred me.

I listened and learned from her to get up, be thankful, and do what I'm supposed to do. Actions come before feelings, that's for sure. My situation was short term, and I did take the medication for a short time, and changed my routine—but the main thing I learned was to be thankful. Thankful for how He made me, and thankful that I now better understand those who don't bounce out of bed and welcome the day. I've incorporated into my daily prayer time a "Thanks-giving" list—listing each day at least three things for which I'm thankful. God has taught me through my easy times, and especially through the struggles. He's in charge of the "glass" and I'm in charge—my choice—of how to see it.

Tweaking Patterns of Thinking

If any of the half-empty comments ring true in your life (thoughts or words), you can tweak what you think. Negative patterns can be replaced with positive ones—it is a choice, a daily one. Fill your mind with God's word, which tells you how much you are loved by him, what plans he has for you (and your family), and how nothing has caught him by surprise. He's in charge, and he loves you with all his heart.

Look at John 3:16. "For God so loved the world that he gave his one and only Son, that whoever believes in him shall not perish but have eternal life."

Now, put *your* name in the verse. I'll insert my name as an example, and whenever I do so, it always brings tears to my eyes and gets things in perspective. "For God so loved *Lynda* that he gave his one and only Son, that if *Lynda* believes in him she shall not perish but have eternal life."

That eternal life starts now, and the Lord stands by your side and gives you strength for each new day (2 Tim. 4:17). Ask him.

You're riding the waves as they slam on the shoreline boulders. Then you catch your breath as the waves recede and you float on the white foam. In the distance, you spot the next breaker building—but for the present minutes, hours, or days, you rest in the calm.

Let God join you in the calm
and the chaos. He's been in both.

Now on to the next chapter that's just for you (or anyone who helps with the care giving in the family.)

Letters floating in your spoon:

C - O - M - F - O - R - T

Your rod and your staff protect and comfort me.

—Psalm 23:4b NLT

Chapter Eight

Caring for the Caregiver

For I know the thoughts I think toward you, says the lord,
thoughts of peace and not of evil, to give you a future and a hope.

—Jeremiah 29:11 NKJV

You may have heard, "If the caregiver goes down the tube, so goes the family," and that's especially true if you have a child with a chronic (ongoing) condition. Your ASD journey is certainly an ongoing situation, and your physical, mental, emotional, and spiritual health are of utmost importance. Many moms say, "I feel guilty taking care of myself." No one else is going to do it. You have a choice, and you need to plan ahead and pray ahead for each day.

On an ASD blog, one mom wrote that she felt so exhausted and on edge that it was like PTSD (Post-Traumatic Stress Disorder). Another mom added that it was more like OTSD—Ongoing-Traumatic Stress Disorder. This chapter is written to give you help, hope, and friendship, like the elephants who wrap trunks as a sign of friendship. Okay, we won't be wrapping trunks, but here are some analogies.

> If the caregiver goes down the tube, so goes the family.

Elephant Analogies

Ignoring the Elephant in the Middle of the Room
Some people avoid talking about their child. They don't use words like "special needs," or give any indication that their child may need extra

help in life. Others notice and may want to help, but if the proverbial elephant in the middle of the room isn't addressed, parents stay in denial and no one is allowed to come alongside.

However, the elephant is still there and it affects the entire family. You and your family need to accept what you know is happening, and be open to help from the outside world—the world outside your home.

You Need To Take "Small Bites of the Elephant"

As a parent, you know you can't handle the entire situation, or, as they say, you can't eat an entire elephant in one sitting—you need to take small bites. To be truthful, there are days you feel like you've bitten off more than you can ever chew, and you're choking.

Slow down, take deep breaths, write down your feelings in your journal, call a friend who "gets it," and take small steps to get all the things that need to get done (the "elephant") under better control. When you've accomplished anything on your list for the day and can mark it off, you feel so much better. Bottom line: prioritize what *really* needs to be done, and simplify your life.

They Say That Elephants Never Forget (But You Do)

You may forget appointments, where you left your keys, and the name of the speech therapist the lady in the line behind you at the grocery store told you yesterday. But your child seems never to forget anything.

"You said you'd take me to . . ."

"Dad said last week that we'd go to . . ."

"My teacher said I could . . ."

And your child is usually correct. Those words have been said, perhaps promised in haste. You may forget, but he won't.

But right now, you still can't find your keys. You can't find anything, but he can, so ask your SC to find them for you. If *anyone* can find them, he can. If he's seen them or heard where they were, he'll remember. And remember to put your keys back on the hook by the door or wherever they should be. Your SC may be at school the next time you lose them.

From Elephants to Endorphins

Stress sends a barrage of negative chemical messengers (adrenaline and cortisol in particular) through the brain, throwing us into a fight or flight mode. We may overreact in anger, or run away from the problem. The results: you hurl hurtful words; you shut down and climb in bed to sleep; you lose yourself on the computer; or you wander and shop at the mall. Bottom line: you don't face the situation, and with an ASD situation, it is a *daily* decision to deal with it.

To combat stress, there is a third choice, one not ruled by your emotions. Your emotions may scream at you, "Fight!" or "Flight!" but you don't have to completely give in to them. Choose to jumpstart the positive messengers in the brain, the endorphins.

Endorphins are chemical transmitters in the brain that attach themselves to the same cell receptors that morphine does. They abolish the sensation of pain. The brain doesn't know if the person is really happy, it just responds to the happy messengers. And, as an added bonus, they boost the immune system. Let's look at some ways we can release some of those precious endorphins.

> The choices you make today impact tomorrow—and the next day, and the next day . . .

Laughter: You may need to start this on your own. What's funny to you? A funny movie, something on the Web, a humorous book? Have a kindergartener tell you a Knock, Knock joke, and when he gets to the punchline, watch him bend over in laughter.

Play: Do something you enjoy doing. Have some fun by your-self, with your family, with friends. Just do something somewhere with someone.

Sleep: Try to get at least six to eight hours of sleep at night. I know what you're thinking: *Like that is ever going to happen.* But do what you can, especially to get that REM (rapid eye movement) toward the end of your sleep cycle (when you're dreaming). You have several cycles of REM sleep, but the last one before you wake is the most beneficial. It refreshes you and gets the endorphins flowing. Turn off the lights, the TV, the computer, and any distraction so your mind can gear down.

Getting your child to go to sleep may be another story, so get some help there, too. Other sleep-deprived families have helpful hints on Web sites and blogs, and check with your doctor and other professionals, also. If your child (or anyone in the family) is a "night" person, it will be much harder to get her to bed—and much harder to get her up in the morning.

"I wish they had night school for elementary-aged children," an exhausted mom said.

---

*"I feel like I have permanent jet lag,
you know, no sleep," a mom said.*

If you need to, take a quick nap in the early afternoon if at all pos-sible. It will help you get through the evening.

Exercise: I know, you're smiling and shaking your head. You're thinking, "When in the world can I do that, or when would I ever have the energy, or even want to exercise?" Well, ten minutes of walking gets the blood flowing through your body and lifts your foggy mind. Do you have a treadmill? Or can you walk in your neighborhood? How about walking fast at Walmart up and down the aisles pushing a basket?

If you have small children, load them up and get outside. The sunshine will help all of you. Vitamin D is deficient in many females, so soak it up. And you can appreciate God's creation, the blue sky, green trees, changing colors, vibrant plants, dirt, and bugs (your ASD child will probably enjoy that more than anything).

Deep Breaths: Breathe precious oxygen in through your nose and to your lungs and out through your mouth, releasing toxins in your body.

Water: Stay hydrated. Also, water flushes out toxins. Keep a water bottle filled and sip on it. It also helps you stay away from all the sweet and caffeinated drinks you may be drawn to.

Prayer: God is always there, and he wants to hear from you. Also, read his word and listen to his heart in John 3:16.

Music: Listen to music that brings you joy. Music stirs our hearts and surfaces our emotions. Sing loud and proud. You spend a great deal of time in the executive details of managing a household, which are "left-brain" jobs. Allow music to give your left brain a break and occupy your "right brain" with something artistic.

> "The Bible is more real than the book you are holding in your hands."
>
> —Brennan Manning

Helpful Hints from Others on the Journey

- Be aware of your own needs.
- Do something. Don't shut down.
- Play to your strengths.
- Fix what you can and let the rest go. Simplify, prioritize, minimize.
- Join or start a support group.

- Plan ahead: Have the name of the computer guy, electrician, plumber, and others ready if needed. Keep your gas tank at least half full.
- Eat a good diet.
- Don't forget that God is thinking about you and loves you.

Take care of yourself, so you can take care of your family. If the caregiver goes down the tube, so goes the family. It isn't being selfish, it's being smart. Remember the instructions they give on an airplane: "Should the cabin lose pressure, oxygen masks will fall from the ceiling in front of you. If you are traveling with small children, *place the mask on yourself first*, then place a mask on your child." There's a reason for that instruction. Take a deep breath.

Letters floating in your spoon:
P - R - E - P - A - R - E

You prepare a feast for me in the presence of my enemies.

—Psalm 23:5a NTL

Chapter Nine

Family Flocks

We cannot change our past . . . we cannot change the fact that people act a certain way. We cannot change the inevitable. The only thing we can do is play on the one string we have, and that is our attitude. I am convinced that life is 10 percent what happens to me and 90 percent how I react to it.

—Charles Swindoll

Flying with the Flocks

Let's consider some lessons from the wobbly V. You hear them before you see them. Suddenly, they swoosh overhead, the wobbly V of Canada geese gliding across the horizon, honking encouragement to one another for their extensive journey. ASD families endure long journeys too, and they desperately need encouragement. Surprisingly perhaps, we can learn from flocks of flying geese. Let these lessons strengthen your weary wings.

In a flock of geese flying in V formation, the lead goose rotates back in the formation when it grows tired. Are you the lead goose? Are you the main caregiver on this journey? If so, you may feel you can never rotate back and must always take the lead. Besides, what would others think if you weren't there all the time? The fact is, dear lead goose, you are on an extremely long journey. Take the opportunity to rotate back at times. Others will need you for the extensive journey.

Canada geese work together as they migrate. Each bird in the V flaps its wings, creating an uplift for the following bird, thereby traveling seventy-one percent further than if each bird flew on its own. Your family flock needs to uplift each other, and it's essential to fly in the same direction. There are a number of ways to make this happen. Your children shouldn't hear conflicting opinions expressed in front of them.

Do your best to communicate your ideas and listen to others' opinions. If you do disagree about strategies for your child(ren), discuss the differences of opinions in private.

Each goose's special "Honk!" inspires courage. "Keep on going! You can do it!" This may entail honking encouragement as you deal with family dynamics and checking on the harmony among family members. In the darkness, geese continue to communicate by honking, so no goose gets lost. By effective communication—talking and listening to each other—no one in the family gets lost in the darkness, and all stay connected.

However, if a goose has to drop out of formation, another goose (or two) drops out and flies alongside it. If it lands to recharge, the other two stay with it until they can all rejoin the flock. There may be times that a member of your family has to drop out of formation owing to health issues, emotional overload, or other hindering circumstances. Others (immediate or extended family) need to be made aware to come alongside until the member is able to join the flock again. Understandably much of the family's time may be directed at the SC, but keep your eyes open for others who require help.

Your family may have had great coping skills in the past; if so, those skills will probably help you. However, this is an entirely new journey. Unlike geese that follow the same migration year after year, you and your flock have not traveled this way before. Individuals' thoughts on issues may change daily—even hourly—so take time each day to share those feelings. Holding them in is counterproductive, but remember to share them in love.

Family "Fotos"

When you planned for your family's future, you assumed all your children would be perfect. That's right. Perfect. Snapshots included a smiling baby who babbles, toddles, walks, and talks at "appropriate" times. She would continue to hit all the marks and would never talk back or fuss. Now, try to find one like that.

But what if the real snapshots of your child include fussiness, lack of babbling, talking, and walking at "appropriate" times, and meltdowns. Extreme meltdowns.

"He isn't perfect, and I don't have a clue what to do!" Parents don't say that out loud, but the thoughts creep in. An extra load of guilt lands if these thoughts emerge: "I don't even like him at times, especially when I'm wrestling him to the ground and he's spitting at me."

No child is perfect, and neither is any parent. But you can be the parent your child needs.

Moms and Dads

"My dad is the boss . . . until Grandma comes over. Then he's just one of us."
—A child in *Kids Say the Greatest Things about God*

"I feel disconnected from the family," a dad said.

Some say that eighty percent of marriages that include a child with autism end in divorce. New studies find that autism divorce rates are similar to families without the disorder (sixty-four percent). One mom said, "If you've had a strong marriage beforehand, the journey will be very challenging; however, you'll have a good chance of making it. However, if things have been rocky beforehand, then the extra stresses of autism may shake the marriage apart."

> Sometimes not making a decision is making the decision. Stay focused.

No matter what the statistics say (or don't say), the choices you make for your journey will determine where you end. Don't be overwhelmed with hopelessness, thinking, "Nothing will help." Positive choices each day *will* help. They'll help your child, your marriage, and yourself.

Family Talks With Your Child

Reduce your words. If he is non-verbal, mildly verbal, or extremely verbal, reduce your language. Here's why:

- He may pick up too many other noises that block your words.
- Use of negatives is a block, as well. He only hears the active verb, so say what you want him to do, not what you don't want. "Walk on your feet," instead of, "Don't run." Also, "Hands to yourself," instead of, "Don't hit."
- He has difficulty picking out the important words. He doesn't read your body language, either.
- He has difficulty sequencing what you've told him. Give simple instructions, and one at a time.

"Doesn't he need to hear more talking to help him talk? What if he falls even farther behind?" Don't worry. Reducing your language will not delay their speech or teach them bad habits. Use concrete terms, and avoid metaphors or ambiguous language.

Start by gaining her attention. Usually start talking to her by saying her name first, even if it is just the two of you. Why? It's important to use her name first to make it very clear you are speaking to her. Using her name will also give her a chance to tune into your voice. Take away "distracters" before talking to her, then speak eye to eye and face to face.

Do not overuse her name, however—it may become like "white noise" if she hears it too much. At first, get her attention by body positioning, using a small environmental noise like a tap to get visual attention, or a gentle leading of the elbow to turn the child in your direction before giving commands.

Delete unnecessary words. Take out all unnecessary words and phrases, and give him time to process what you have just said. You may have to wait an unusually long time before speaking again to give him time to make sense of what you've said. You may not like the awkward silence, but if you rephrase your question again too quickly, he may have to start processing what you have said all over again and become frustrated. Also, you may end up answering *for* your child.

So, for example, instead of saying, "It's time to put your shoes on, Jamison. We are going to the park to feed the ducks. Put your cars away now. Come on, quickly," you could say, "Jamison, we are going to the park. Put your shoes on." Show him his shoes and a picture of the park (to ensure he really understands what you are saying to him). Give him the picture to hold, as a reminder.

> Remember, he needs the time lapse to translate your words so he can understand what's been said.

When his shoes are on, say, "Let's go to the park." Then wait. The child heard you say it, and he will do it, but it might take a couple of seconds or minutes longer to register.

When it's time to leave the park, give him a five-minute warning, another at three minutes, and then, "Time to go," with a picture of where you're going next. Pictures for each phase will help so much. Use a "transitional object" for him to hold, such as a ball to take home, and then when he gets home, remind him that it is his responsibility to put the ball in his room. Step by step by step by step. . . .

This "first . . . then" language is used with many children on the spectrum, and it works with typical children, too. In classrooms, the system is used so a child knows what comes next on the schedule. Sometimes (and it can be done different ways) a file folder is divided down the center with a line. On one side is written FIRST, with a piece of Velcro underneath, and on the other side is written THEN, with another piece of Velcro. That way, throughout the day, pictures can be placed in the two spots showing the child, for example, FIRST math, THEN gym. Or, FIRST wash hands, THEN lunch. This method can be used anywhere as you get ready for transitions.

Grandparents

"Over the river and through the woods, to grandmother's house we go."

Planting Seeds for Future Generations

Grandparents are one generation removed from the SC, and they have the potential for giving unconditional love. "We see our grandchildren through a different set of lenses than their parents—more like what they are inside."

> *"We worry about our adult child and about our grandchild. Double worrying, I guess you'd call it," a grandmother said.*

Grandparents, you have the special privilege of planting seeds of encouragement in the lives of all your grandchildren—and some desperately need those seeds. When the world taunts them because they are different (and not in a good way), you come alongside with the truth that they are precious children with so much to offer the world.

Visits at Grandparents' House

Your grandchild may be coming to your house for a visit, or your grandchild may live with you in your house. Here are some helpful hints (house rules) that will make the visit or living situation more positive for you, whoever lives with you, and for your grandchild.

Using visual supports to give your grandchild extra "cues" is important. Most people on the spectrum are visual learners, so when talking to your grandchild, show them a visual cue (picture), as well. A younger child may need to be shown an actual object first; later, you may be able to move on to photographs, black-and-white line drawings, and then words. SCs often need visual cues to remind them what they are doing, how long activities will last, and what they are going to do next.

Using pictures to help communicate will not stop speech development. Using pictures will give your grandchild a better chance of understanding you and lower anxiety levels. Gestures and sign language are fantastic bridges to communication, as well.

Having a timetable at your house with pictures of the activities for your grandchild to complete will help them to know what is expected of them. For example, you could have five pictures: toys, book with grandma or grandpa, snacks, video, and home. These pictures could change depending on what you are doing during each visit, although always keep the "home" picture as the last symbol so they can see when the visit has finished and where they are going next.

Going to Your Grandchild's House

You may sometimes go to your grandchild's house to look after them. Be sure to keep the same routine they have with their parents. This may need to be written down for you so you know the exact order in which the routine happens; for example, does your grandchild have a drink before a bedtime story, or do they have a favorite CD to listen to in bed?

Does a certain light need to be left on? Your grandchild will also need to go to bed at the same time. For some children, a change in routines can lead to high levels of anxiety and, in turn, difficult behaviors.

Your grandchild will also need to be shown that you are coming to care for them that evening. For example, one of their parents could show them a photo of you and add it to their daily timetable. They will also need to reassure them, again, visually, that they are coming back at the end of the evening.

Concrete-thinking Grandchildren

No matter what you've accomplished in life, your concrete-thinking grandchild takes you at face value. In the heartwarming book *Dancing with Max*, Emily Colson shares her journey with her son, Max. Emily's father, Chuck Colson, shares this story of one special day with his grandson.

Whenever Max arrives at our house he skips through the rooms taking inventory to make sure nothing has been moved since his last visit. He finds security and comfort in routines and familiar surroundings. One place he almost always stops is my ego wall—yes, I admit I have one—where there are pictures of me with various luminaries collected over the years. Max stands at that wall and rattles off the names of the people I'm pictured with. "Grandpa and President Bush . . . Grandpa and the pope . . . Grandpa and Billy Graham. . . ." And on and on he goes through every picture on the wall.

We have placed one restriction on Max, however: he is never to touch the switches for the ceiling fans. The reason is simple. He is obsessed with motors and household appliances.

If he were to turn the fan on and off several times in rapid sequence it would burn out the motor. He knows that it's Grandpa's job to turn on the fans.

When Max returned to school after a visit, one of his teachers asked him to tell his class about his trip to Florida. He immediately recited all the pictures on the wall. The teacher called Emily to ask if Max was making this up—did her father really know all those people? Emily explained that I had served in the White House. So the next day they questioned Max standing in the front of the class: "What was your grandfather's job at the White House?"

Max quickly responded, "He turned on the fans."

All in perspective.

Fighting Fatigue

You may be so worn out worrying about your child (the parent), your grandchild, and his siblings, that you forget about taking care of yourself. You've given your time and energy over the years in raising your child, and now you're giving again. Turn to Chapter Eight, "Caring for the Caregiver," for tips on coping with compassion fatigue. You are a vital part of the caregiving team.

Financial Frustrations

"We want to help our daughter financially with the mounting treatment bills for our grandchild, or put money in a special trust for later—but can't even help with the everyday expenses of the now," a grandmother said.

You can only do what you can do. The main thing your adult child needs from you is your emotional support. Whatever you can give physically or any other way is an added blessing.

Primary Caregivers

"My husband has put off retirement, and he works extra hours for more money. I'm at home and deal with the meltdowns and endless tasks to care for our grandchild. And no matter how you cut it, our bodies are getting older—slower—and we don't have the strength to cope with a child who is taller than we are and certainly stronger than I."

"My friends don't understand why I can't do what they do. They *want* to understand, but can't. They don't live my life 24/7. I can't even sneak out for a quick lunch with my friends—and getting a babysitter is almost impossible. *I'm* the babysitter!"

Grandparents who are the primary caregivers (or even secondary) voice concerns about their own health as they get older. Also, who will help with their grandchild in the future, and what happens when they die? These aren't issues that anyone wants to discuss, but if you plan ahead and put things in writing, it will take some of the burden off your shoulders now.

Extended Family

Aunt: "Jason's only three; he'll talk. You're just overreacting."

Parent: "Yes, Jason's only three, but we think there are some things we need to look into."

Uncle: "Sarah is five; you were a little weird as a kid, too. Don't worry about it."

Parent: "Yes, I remember you kidded me—but this is different, Uncle Charley."

Grandfather: "We've never had anything on our side of the family." (Glances at the other grandfather). "Micah's fine."

Parent: "I know, Dad, we've never dealt with this before, but we're dealing with it now, and we need your support. We need *everyone's* support."(Glances around the room at family.)

Extended family may not understand your journey, but many times they can be a valuable source of help. They have to be educated just like everyone else who is on your journey.

Truthful Talks with the Family

- Establish facts: What is happening in the family now? Using correct names and treatments makes each family member more comfortable and relaxed and decreases second guessing.
- Establish plans: How will the family deal with things in the future (as much as you know now). Plan ahead for your new normal. Does your family need to get to a family picnic, a function at school or church, or wherever there's transition and adjustment, a little earlier than others? Transitions usually become easier over time, and fewer triggers are important. But for now, get there early, take what you need to cope, and be ready to leave if needed.
- Establish togetherness: Everyone is on this family team, and all are adjusting to your your new normal.
- New normal together: No one is alone, and all are valued and heard. You share each other's strengths and help with weaknesses.

Your SC may be exhausted from holding it together while in public, and then meltdown hits when he gets to the car and/or home. Realize that others in the family have held it together in public (more like holding their breaths), as well, and they need to emotionally let down in the car and/or at home.

Everyone is on the spectrum roller coaster, and everyone needs some down time when you pull into the gate at the end of the ride. The siblings probably don't realize the exhaustion a parent may feel, because the adult doesn't show how the "ride" outside the home has affected him or her. Some knowledge of this is a good thing for the siblings, so you might say, "I know we'll all be tired when we get home tonight, so let's plan ahead what each of us can do to make it a good transition at home before bedtime. What are some of your ideas?"

Flying Through The Holidays

Merry Christmas!
(From Colleen Swindoll Thompson's blog.)

How many of you feel comfortable talking about depression? Better yet, do you share your convictions when someone else is vulnerable about being depressed?

Let me start off by stating that depression can be a severe struggle for parents raising special-needs children. Depression can be indescribable, grievous, and debilitating. It's not easy to talk about! I know because I've struggled with depression for years. I have questioned whether life is worth living and have doubted all of life's meaning in the darkness. If you are suffering, my heart breaks for you. I pray that God provides His mercy to you in abundance, particularly throughout this time of year.

During the holidays, as many special-needs families encounter increased struggles, depression becomes an even greater possibility. Even "normal" things, like buying presents and going to events—the regular unraveling of schedules—can be very discouraging throughout the season. When my son Jon was six, his Christmas list included: a washing machine, fans of all shapes and sizes, a vacuum cleaner, and a waterfall in his room. Such are the highlights of holidays! It's humorous to me now, but it wasn't when he was six and I was longing to give him presents like the ones I imagined other parents giving their children. More than that, my wish to give him what no human ever could was only accentuated.

So, I know what a struggle depression can be, especially around the holidays. I know and I want this season to be a great one for you. Here are some things I've done that have positively affected my attitude and perspective. I encourage you to choose a few of these ideas to help you enjoy a delightful holiday season this year.

- Journal about your emotions and struggles with candid honesty. Emotions are necessary to your life . . . but so is having a healthy outlet for exploring and expressing them so that they don't end up mastering your life and damaging your direction.

- Allow a few very trustworthy friends to know what you're going through and support you. You aren't alone, though it's easy to feel like you are. Reach out and let people who love you help you.

- Reach out and help someone else. Organize a room in your house and clear away clutter. Offer usable items that you no longer need to a family who does.
- Reflect on the people in your life and actively give thanks for them. Write a note to those whom you respect, listing the wisdom you gleaned from your time with them.
- Remind yourself of your value in God's eyes and the gifts He has given you through your struggles. Put together a book for yourself that celebrates your identity in Christ and His power in your life. When you flip through the pages, you'll be able to see very clearly what He has already done and what He promises He will do.

I pray these ideas will help guard your heart against depression this year and help you experience the peace and presence of Immanuel, God with us, in this and every season.

We began this chapter with Chuck Swindoll's statement about our attitude. We'll end with one of his also, "Each day of our lives we make deposits in the memory banks of our children."

Someone in the next chapter is waiting for your deposit their memory bank—the siblings.

Letters floating in your spoon:
B - L - E - S - S - I - N - G - S

You honor me by anointing my head with oil.
My cup overflows with blessings.

—Psalm 23:5b NTL

Chapter Ten

Siblings—The "Invisible" Ones

*If you're the sibling of an ASD kid, you're called "typical," but you
really aren't—because you aren't typical like anyone else you know.*

—Anna Geary, a sibling

A Beautiful Once

Mom came home today, crying.
Dad too, and he held her hand.
They had been to the doctor with you,
A routine checkup only.
I'd never thought twice about it.
Why you didn't talk in English,
How your speech wasn't words.
It always made sense to me.
Or how you liked to flap your hands in the air.
I thought in celebration,
But really trying to grasp a bit of normalcy.
Or the way you loved to spin in circles,
Over, over, over.
Round, round, round.
It seemed like fun to me.
These silly pleasures of childhood,
They will forever be a drug,
Soothing the wires in your brain that are crossed.
Not badly,
Just differently.
Connections, nerve impulses
Firing in a way we can't understand.
Sweet baby brother,
We thought you'd outgrow it,
And we giggled at your eccentricities.
Never once thinking this was permanent.

"Autism" was never in our vocabulary,
No one told us about the Spectrum
Where you fall somewhere, 1 in every 150.
There is no cure, no magic pill.
Just "progress."
But, today, I made you a promise.
Breathed it in your ear in a moment of peace
I made sure no one looked.
I'll love you always,
Do my best to make you understand.
Somehow you comprehended my words,
A moment of clarity in clouded eyes.
Defied the disease,
And wrapped an arm around my shoulder.
Physical touch not driving you wild for a beautiful once.

—Anna Geary, teenage sibling
(aaronbridge.org)

The Eyes Have It

Want to know what someone is *really* thinking? Watch their eyes. Newscasters on TV show their "professional face" as they interview people—but then a story hits their heart, and the sparkle in their eyes fades. The smile may remain, but the eyes tell another story. Mute the sound on your TV and watch people's eyes.

That's what you see many times in a family with a special-needs or chronically/critically ill child. Sometimes people swoop in on TV with lots of energy to rebuild their house; or the family is interviewed on a special TV program relating to the child; even children in poverty who have been the draw for help receive special medical devices or operations. All these things are wonderful as people come alongside.

But I notice the siblings standing nearby, not pushed to the side on purpose, but they don't *need* any extra help. They are just there, and I always wonder what they're thinking and feeling. You see one lifting his sister with cerebral palsy into a wheelchair, or chasing a younger autistic brother before he bolts out the door, or simply staring at the cameras as he sits quietly at the end of the couch with his family.

We need to focus on and help children in need, absolutely, but we also need to be aware of the "invisible" ones—the siblings. They may be babies who will grow up with their family's challenges as a normal life. Or they may continue to adjust to ongoing changes in their family as they watch their ASD sibling cope with her struggles. Or they may be an older sibling, worried about their worn-out parents and what their role will be in the future.

> National Siblings Day is April 10! Plan something special for the sibling(s) in your family.

Your ASD child may labor with reading body language and nuances from your typical child(ren). However, *you* will learn much from your typical child's words, body language, and especially his eyes. Keep the communication lines open and remember who she is—another one of your precious children, unique in her own right with needs of her own. And don't be fooled by an independent child. They have needs too.

Sibs' Statistics

The spectrum statistics are staggering. One in every ninety-one children in the United States is on the autistic spectrum. A new case is diagnosed every twenty minutes, and there are 24,000 new cases each year. The total? More than one million individuals in the United States are on the spectrum, according to the Centers for Disease Control and Prevention, the American Academy of Pediatrics, and other federal agencies.

These beloved "statistics" live in your home and in your heart. Not only is your child with ASD one of those statistics impacted by autism, but so are the other siblings in the family. All are affected and all are finding their way on this journey. You are there for all of them—and we are here to come alongside in helping your family pull together.

Sibs' Roles

Throughout their lives, typical brothers and sisters may play many different roles in the lives of their ASD siblings, and they will be in their lives *longer than anyone.*

"Our biggest worry is the long-term care our child will need. We're fairly certain he'll outlive us—and we want the best care and life for him—but we also want the best life for our other children, especially if they end up being his caregivers," a dad said. "We're trying to make plans for those issues, and have his siblings be a part of the discussion with their input as they get older."

Sibs' Personalities

- **Overachiever sibs:** Some typically developing brothers and sisters react to their siblings' disability by setting unrealistically high expectations for themselves, and they feel they must compensate for their siblings' special needs. Parents, you can help by conveying clear expectations and *unconditional support.*
- **Why-bother sibs:** These sibs slip into the shadows hoping you'll not ask them to do anything. If they can keep a low profile and simply be connected to their iPod (or whatever gadget they use), they won't have to deal with the situation

at home. "No one knows if I'm there or not anyway," one said.

- **Go-with-the-flow sibs:** She's there, she'll help if needed, and she'll adjust to anyone's schedule. But don't take her for granted—remember, she has needs, also. She can get lost in the shuffle, so remember to call her by name. She may not hear it that much.

- **Fifty-best-friends sibs:** She knows everyone and everyone knows her. She'll help when needed, but be sure other people (her peer group) are included, if possible. Don't expect her to remember details, though, or where you left your keys. (Review Resource One, You-Niquely Made Personality Study)

Sibling Rivalry

"This sounds crazy, but I'm glad to see our kids arguing. It makes our family seem normal. Our typical child is standing up for what he wants to do, and our ASD child may not understand, but there's beginning to be some give and take—arguing, but some give and take," a mom said.

When conflict arises, the message sent to many typical brothers and sisters is, "Leave your sibling alone. You are bigger, you are stronger, you should know better. It is your job to compromise." Typically developing siblings deserve a life where they, like other children, sometimes misbehave, get angry, and fight with their siblings.

Children need to know from their parents' deeds and words that their parents care about them as individuals. When parents carve time out of a busy schedule to grab a bite at a local burger joint or window shop at the mall with their typically developing children, it conveys a message that parents "are there" for them, as well, and provides an excellent opportunity to talk about a wide range of topics.

Celebrate Sibs

You are so excited about every achievement and milestone that your ASD child hits, yes, celebrate! But don't overlook their sibling's milestones. High school graduations, soccer games, piano recitals, and even weddings can be missed if plans aren't made in advance to be there. Don't give in to, "We just didn't make it because we couldn't get a sitter." "She'll understand," doesn't cut it, either. She may have "understood" all the things you missed while she was growing up, but it is so important to her that you be there, whether she says so or not.

> It's important to be more than (ASD) Suzanne's sister.

Don't let challenging issues dictate your life. Plan ahead and seek respite resources, strive for flexibility, and seek creative solutions that can help assure that the accomplishments of all family members are celebrated. There are many resources on the web for siblings such as SibNet.

Viewpoints

Siblings are individuals with unique personalities, interests, and their own place in your family's birth order. They need help to cope and carve out their own identity.

Parents, do whatever it takes to keep communication open with these siblings. Remember that each of you sees things from your point of view.

Siblings may think:

- "My parents don't have enough energy to take care of themselves, much less me."
- "I don't want to resent Marcus, but I do—and I don't know what to do with those feelings."

- "People feel sorry for me, and I appreciate that, but I don't want pity, I want to be seen as a person."

Parents may think:

- "I can't meet all the needs of our autistic son, as well as our other three children."
- "I don't know what our autistic child is thinking, as well as most of the time, I don't know what our typical child is thinking—he clams up."
- "As long as the sibling doesn't demand attention, I think things are okay. I've found out that isn't true."

Give Age-Appropriate Information

A young sibling's world has consisted of living with an older ASD brother or sister. This is all the younger sibling knows. However, he needs your personal talks with him at times about ASD—and about his feelings.

Young Sibs

If you feel your child is old enough to even partially understand that your spectrum child is "special" or different from other children, then tell her, but give the child only as much information as you feel she can handle. One way you may wish to explain autism or the spectrum to your child is to say, "Autism makes your brother/sister special; it makes him/her think differently from most people." Accentuate your spectrum child's positive qualities and gifts.

Often, these children are more understanding and accepting than we think, and they'll find ways to communicate and play with your other child. So make it part of your child's therapy plan to include his or her siblings in activities. Ask your child's therapy team to make a goal for appropriate sibling interaction. This will not only help your spectrum child in communication and interaction, it will help your typical child learn how to interact. Often, siblings pick up on many techniques and cues from therapists and become "little therapists" themselves. Many times, they translate your ASD child's wants and words.

Teen Sibs

> Choose your battles—keep communication open with your teen

The teenage years are difficult; that's a fact. Most typical teens experience the "It's all about me" stage during these years. The hormones kick in, and your compliant elementary school–aged child seems to have disappeared. (Unless, of course, you have a very compliant teen—and in that case, you can skip the rest of this section—or, you may want to read on, because you just never know.)

As children mature, some emotions crop up in typical teens as they deal with their ASD siblings: anger, embarrassment, and guilt. They are angry at having a brother or sister with a disability that forces them to make sacrifices, they are embarrassed about their sibling's behavior, and they feel guilty for being the typical one—and for all the above thoughts.

How do you help your teen cope? First and foremost, realize this is a difficult journey for your typical child, and adolescence can be an incredibly difficult time. Be calm and understanding, and try to realize that this is very normal. Second, keep reiterating to your typical child that autism (or spectrum) was not a choice, it was nobody's fault, and that you are and will always remain a family.

> His feelings are real to him. Validate that.

If your teen continues to feel angry or depressed, he may be in need of more help than you can provide. You may want to consider family or psychological counseling for your typical child to help him deal with these feelings. Often, an unbiased outside source can provide tremendous help and insight and validate your child's feelings.

Communication

That must mean talking, right? Not really. Keep in mind that communication is ninety-two percent body language, eye contact, and tone of voice.

Be Open and Honest

Be honest from the start about your ASD child's situation. Communicate on the sibling's level. She will learn that she can trust your word now and in the future. Children are smarter than we tend to think, and they know that something "just isn't right." This often translates into feelings of guilt and they blame themselves, especially if they are young, because they think everything revolves around them and they must have caused it. Talk about their feelings and clear up misunderstandings.

> Your concern for your child is caught not taught.

Misunderstandings

Young children are a wealth of misinformation. They hear lots of new words that they are translating into their world, just as your ASD child is doing to a much greater degree. Listen to the siblings talk, especially to their friends. You might pick up things that need to be corrected.

"My mom said my brother has asparagus!"
Asperger's misunderstood—again.

Keep Others in the Loop

> Prayers for those involved: Lord, thank you for all those involved in my child's life. Give them wisdom, love, and strength for all the duties they have and all the lives they touch. Amen.

This includes your child's teachers, coaches, scout leaders, and anyone connected with your child who needs to know what is happening in your home. The amount of information and who to tell is your decision, but the more they know, and the more they know how to help your child, the better off for everyone.

These "others" may not even know there *is* a loop to be "in," and they may not understand your typical child's coping mechanisms, such as acting out behavior, or falling grades. They may have heard something in passing from another teacher or friend, but they need to hear from you about how you want issues to be handled. That will help them more than you know.

Emotional Landmines

Emotion builds up and explodes—either outside your child, or inside. Everyone needs an outlet.

Anger

"When he hits me it really hurts, then when I try to protect myself, I'm the one who gets in trouble," a sibling said.

Encourage your child to write in a diary or journal, or draw pictures of how she feels. It's a safe place to vent anger. Encourage physical activity. Have her run around the yard, shoot baskets, climb on a playground, or beat clay. Be sure and let her know that you will not let her be hurt. Home is a safe place.

Jealousy

"My mom spends all her time with Andrew, at home, going to the therapists, night and day."

Your child may have difficulty understanding why their SC sibling gets to do things that they can't do, such as spend time with a therapist. Making special time for you and your typical child or children is important.

If your child is young, schedule "Mommy and Me" times during which the two of you play games, color, or participate in enjoyable activities together. Make sure your child knows that you are available to have your own "special time." Get a sitter, if you can, or ask your spouse to stay home while you take your other child out, or simply hide away together in a room in the house. Make sure this is time to do what your child wants to do (if possible), *not what you think needs to be done*. It makes your child feel special, and it will ease your mind considerably.

Frustration

"People only ask my parents about my sister. I'm still here, aren't I?"

Suggest to your friends and family that they ask about your typical child first and what's happening in her life; then, ask about your spectrum child.

> Validate the sibling's feelings. They're real.

Embarrassment

"My brother crawls under the table when we're out to eat, and he eats off the floor before my mom can grab him. You ought to see how the people look at us. I just want to crawl under the table myself and *stay* there."

Plan a time when you get home and things are settled down to "catch up" with your typical child. Let her express how she felt about an embarrassing situation. Brainstorm things that might be done the next time

155

to help. When she knows she's not the only one feeling embarrassed, she will not feel so alone.

> *"Even though my brother is really weird at times, when someone makes fun of him it hurts me a lot. He's still my brother."*

Loneliness

"We're all in the house together, so why do I feel so alone?"

Spend time, time, and more time with your child.

"I don't have any time, much less *more* time to spend with my child(ren)," a mom said.

Plan ahead and carve out the time—small segments will do. Ask your child *when* he feels lonely and what you can do about it. Keep daily routines as "routine" as possible. "Routine?" you say. Yes, even your ravaged routines can have some order, but it takes everyone in the family working toward that end.

> *"Mom, I'll take care of Mikey in the store for you. You'll just get mad and yell at him and it makes things worse," a typical sibling said.*

Fear

"I'm afraid of my brother—especially when he bites or hits me. He's getting bigger and stronger, and I don't know what will set him off."

Talk about these fears with your child and make a plan to give him security, reminding him that you won't let anything happen to him. He doesn't have to take the abuse, even though your spectrum child doesn't know what he's doing. Your typical child needs protection and for home to be a safe place for him.

Your ASD child may have several therapists who work with his challenges. Your typical child may need help, too, emotionally. If a counselor or trusted friend is needed, please be open to getting that help. Yes, the bills are piling up, but that kind of help will have lifelong benefits.

Spiritual Questions

"Why is my sister like she is? Did God make a mistake?"

After wrestling in prayer and reading the Bible, the following are some words written on a blog by a sibling, from God's perspective. "Why do you toil and fret that your sister may be nothing more than she is? Why in your mind do you set her up for failure? Let her be whose she was created to be. Let Me use her as I have planned. And don't grieve in the thought that she has not been accounted for in my plan."

Filling Emotional Tanks

Show your children you love them by filling those emotional tanks again and again. What are their "love languages?" (see Resource One.) Here are some ways to show your love and fill those empty tanks.

- Touch: This includes hugs for teens, too, or just a slight tap on the arm as you pass by.
- Time: Stop, look (eye to eye), and *listen*. Don't just mumble, "Uh huh." Ask where your typical child would like to spend time with you. Then do it.
- Talk: Encouraging words give courage to keep on keeping on. Your typical child may get daily doses of discouraging words in life.

- Gifts: They don't have to be particularly expensive, just something to say, "I'm thinking about you." Choose something meaningful just for them.
- Deeds: What do the children do? Thank them for those acts, and find things to do for them.

Helpful books by Gary Chapman are *Five Love Languages of Children*, and *Five Love Languages of Teenagers*. They make good reading when you can carve out a few minutes—well worth your time.

Dear Reader, as you hold this book in your hands, rest assured you have been prayed for by the author and fellow travelers. You and your family are important to us. We pray that these words encourage you as you affect the lives of your children, whether on the spectrum, not on the spectrum, or anywhere in between. We pray that God will sweep away the fog and give you clarity of view for each child and strength to meet their needs—one step at a time. Again, you are precious to us and more so to him. He is the one who gives us those who come alongside.

"And the peace of God, which surpasses all understanding, will guard your hearts and minds through Jesus Christ."

—Philippians 4:7 NKJV

Letters floating in your spoon:

G-O-O-D-N-E-S-S

Surely your goodness and unfailing love
will pursue me all the days of my life.

—Psalm 23:6a NLT

Chapter Eleven

Friends—The Family You Choose

*A friend is someone who reaches for your hand
but touches your heart.*

—Anonymous

This chapter has two parts. The first deals with *your* friends—those people who keep you afloat. The second part deals with *your child's* friends. They keep your child (and you) afloat, even if your child doesn't express that feeling.

Your Friends

One mom said, "Let me tell you about my special friend—she's my kindred spirit. She called to ask if she could go with me when I get my hair cut. She knows I can't leave my child with a babysitter (even her), and she really knows what will happen at the shop, even for a short time. So, she wants to go along and keep him occupied. She knows how to use my 'emergency kit' as well as I. What a blessing she is."

"Blessed are they who have the gift of making friends, for it is one of God's best gifts. It involves many things, but above all, the power of going out of one's self, and appreciate whatever is noble and loving in another." —Helen Keller

---

Strength and Support

Like an elastic bandage wrapped snuggly around a sprained ankle, giving support during the healing process, so friends wrap around you and provide support during your healing process as you deal with your child's journey. Friends don't squeeze too tight and smother you, but they do give you strength as you continue to function. Allow them that privilege. Don't let them miss the blessing.

Friends are "family," not by blood or marriage, but by love. Sometimes they're closer than relatives, in location and in relationships. They help you carry the burden and get the job done. They bring so many positives into a difficult situation. Many parents noted that friends bring food, pick up the siblings and transport them to and from extracurricular activities, and even take them out for fun activities. They bring groceries and put them away, lug in cleaning supplies to scrub toilets, and throw in a load of wash. Friends also provide spiritual support and prayer.

One mom said, "No matter how bad things have gotten, just being with these church 'sisters' helps me remember that this world isn't the end." Another said, "I have to set limits on how long I unload on some friends. I can completely drain them without realizing it."

"Some people come into our lives and quickly go. Some stay for awhile and leave footprints on our hearts. And we are never, ever the same." —Anonymous

---

Then there are those friends who visit at inconvenient times—for them. You know they've left family at home, left work undone, but they choose to be with you, and you are thankful to have them at your side.

Root Wrapping

Majestic redwoods grow in groups of five and their shallow roots intertwine. This enables those huge trees to survive the severe storms that blow in from the Pacific. Like redwoods, spectrum families "root wrap," enabling them to survive severe storms. Root wrapping starts when you connect with another spectrum family. You almost breathe a sigh of relief knowing that they will understand your journey (at least as much as anyone can). You'll continue to connect with others through support groups, chat rooms, emails, and phone calls. You don't have much time for intertwining, but every little bit helps.

"Happiness is an unexpected hug." —Anonymous

"This is a club that none of us wanted to join, but you are relieved when someone understands the unwritten and unspoken 'rules.' It's a bizarre world with a secret language." Here's what some parents say about the club:

- There's no president; it's all equal opportunity, no matter what you have or don't have. Some families are wealthy; some have absolutely nothing of this world's goods. But all families feel the same helplessness when they hear the diagnosis.
- There's no secretary, but you need to keep your own daily journal, including meds (if your child uses them), reactions to the meds, daily charts and schedules, and on it goes. You are your child's best advocate.
- There's no treasurer; all the money is out-go, not income—except from generous friends and organizations. Ask the social workers and other professionals to help you locate organizations and help if needed. Some of the Web

sites listed at the end of the book have suggestions and links that may help.

No one ever looks forward to welcoming new members, but there's an upside—others who *really* understand and encourage you.

Some of you have just joined this club, others have been members a short while, and others for as long as you can remember.

"It's amazing how giving brings such huge returns. We don't do it for that, but it just works that way. Welcome to the club."

"Praise be to . . . the God of all comfort, who comforts us in all our troubles, so that we can comfort those in any trouble with the comfort we ourselves have received from God." —2 Corinthians 1:3–4

It Was the Best of Times; It Was the Worst of Times . . .

There are no mind readers, so you have to let your friends know how you are feeling. You need to tell them there are times you want to talk and times you do not. There will be times you want those close friends to get messages to others, and times you want them to keep them to themselves. There will be times you want to hear about their "normal" lives and times you do not. There will be times you want to hear about their problems and times you do not. Only you can tell someone what you need at any given moment. One mom suggested pinning on a situation-appropriate button: "Thanks, but I don't want to talk now," or "Please let me talk and cry—but just listen."

"A friend hears the song in my heart and sings when my memory fails." —Anonymous

---

Take a few moments to think about the "coincidences" God has brought into your life on this journey. Who are the new friends you're root wrapping with? What have they done for you? What have you had the opportunity to do for them? Thank him for his coincidences, and for all the others God will bring into your life and your child's life in the future. Now, meet more new friends in the new place.

Support Groups

"I cried today at McDonalds," Barbara said.

"You too? I thought I was the only one who let down there," Carolyn said. The group of moms shook their heads and laughed—tired laughs.

Barbara continued, "I'm so stressed out being at home all the time with my son, Anthony. My husband leaves for work at six, and doesn't get home 'til nine." She looked down at her shoes and mumbled, "I sometimes wonder if that's on purpose."

The others let out an audible sigh.

"Don't get me wrong, I love my son. But it's like living on an island all day with these weird rules that don't apply to other people. Thinking, thinking, all the time, trying to figure out beforehand what will set him off, or what has already happened to set him off."

"I know," Barbara continued, "Your brain never shuts down—you're always in crisis-planning mode. There are times I just can't seem to breathe. I'm always thinking, 'Do I try to drive down another street, not the one we usually take from school to home, to avoid a wreck I heard about?'"

Johanna broke into the conversation, saying, "You know, those detours usually bring on endless

> Appreciate the new kindred spirits you wouldn't have met otherwise. They *get it* when you tell your stories, and they nod their heads, roll their eyes, and a slight smile breaks across their face, or they give a knowing little laugh.

questions and meltdowns. I have to navigate our daily journey to avoid alternate routes and detours."

Again, nervous laughter, and total agreement. They all *get it*.

"Laughter is the shortest distance between friends." —Anonymous

---

Appreciate the new opportunities for friends around the world: the internet, support groups, blogs, and Web sites. We didn't have this several years ago.

Later, when Barbara and Bill were propped up in bed, watching TV, she said, "It was such a relief to talk to people who get it. You know, they also have husband and wife's support groups—and they really aren't scary."

Bill snaps, "I didn't say it was scary; I think it's just stupid. And I don't need a group; I have you to talk to. We have each other and that's enough."

Barbara blinks back tears, thinking, *It isn't enough for me.* "I'm going to keep going to the support group."

Both roll over, but sleep doesn't come.

Your Child's Friends

You as a typical person choose, interact with, and express your feelings toward those you call "friend." Your child may not choose, interact with, or express his feelings in any of the same ways, but he wants and needs friends. It is up to you to encourage others to be his friends, to help them bridge the gap with him, and to set up situations that will facilitate these things.

"My son, Rusty, had a friend at school, Stephen, who was typical. Stephen really tried to be his friend, and went out of his way to sit with him and try to enter his world. Then his family moved away, and I thought Rusty didn't care because he didn't 'show' it. Years later, he verbalized how devastated he was when Stephen left. I wished we talked about it more, and even kept in contact some way."

It takes time and effort to connect with your friends, and even more to keep your child connected with his friends. All the time and effort are worth it.

"Let each of you look out not only for his own interests, but also for the interests of others." —Philippians 2:4 NKJV

A Friend's Prayer Answered

In 1975, our friends Jessie and Jarrett welcomed their precious six-month-old adopted son from Korea. They named him Joel. As he grew, his gait was a concern, and Jessie was referred to an orthopedic specialist—seventy-five miles away—to check out his flat feet.

"I walked in thinking I'd hear about corrective shoes, and therapy—but after checking Joel's feet and gait, the doctor said, 'Oh, he has cerebral palsy. See you in three months. 'Bye,' and he walked out the door. I knew nothing about cerebral palsy (CP), and thoughts of the most extreme cases I'd seen flooded my mind as I carried my smiling son to the car and started the seventy-five-mile drive back home—in a daze. He didn't even give me a pamphlet.

"Later, our pediatrician sat down and talked to us, and gave us information about CP. It was caused by lack of oxygen to the brain at birth, it wasn't progressive, and we got far more than a pamphlet—we got hope," Jessie added.

Carol, their neighbor, suggested a free federal program that provided a battery of tests. There was no clear diagnosis, but multiple handicaps were noted that made Joel eligible for services.

True or False

• Children on the spectrum don't want friends. They like to be left alone and live in their own world. False.

• Making and maintaining friendships often proves to be difficult. The *quality* of friendships, not the *quantity* of friends, predicts how lonely they are. True.

"Everyone knew there were problems, but no names could be given; however, we were referred to Easter Seals, with occupational therapy, and later to Carl Sandburg School for special education. I struggled with the idea of a special class, afraid he'd pick up more behaviors to make him even more different. However, the school was perfect for him—the teaching, therapies, and mainly the encouragement from caring teachers and staff. It was like an extended family."

In the second grade, Joel talked to a girl who was to have surgery—a very scared little girl. Joel asked if he could pray for her, which he did right there. He then said, "You'll be okay, because I prayed for you." Later that day, her mother called Jessie and said, "My daughter had been petrified of this upcoming surgery, but after Joel prayed for her and told her it would be okay because he'd prayed for her, she was fine. I just wanted to call and let you know that."

That's how Joel has always been. He believes God is so close, and you talk to him right then—at school or anywhere.

Because Joel had a phenomenal memory for certain items, but struggled in other tasks, Jessie named his condition "Scattergun Diagnosis." She figured parts of his brain worked very well, and other parts didn't—"Lack of oxygen at birth, I think," she said.

Another precious baby from Korea was added to their family—this time a baby girl who they named Joy. Their family was complete.

When Joel was seven, Jessie called several close friends to meet one Saturday morning in our pastor's office to pray for Joel. "This has been on my heart, and I just want Joel to be healed—however God chooses to do that. Not so much for the physical, but an inner healing, because I want him to grow up and be happy," she told the group sitting in a circle. Joel was used to his family praying, and he joined in. His prayers were from his heart, and the cadence of his voice was like Jarrett's voice. We all joined hands and agreed with this family's heart desire for Joel.

Several years passed, and the family moved from Maryland to Idaho and settled in. "Joel needed more of a challenge, and it came in the form of the special education teacher who helped Joel with his classes as needed—a perfect fit. He graduated from high school, and attended the local college."

Sadness struck the family when Jarrett began his battle with cancer. The family pulled together even tighter as they ministered to him before he died. But Jarrett's voice could still be heard in Joel's voice and words.

Joel graduated from college and volunteers whenever anyone asks. He attends every town hall meeting, and he attends church every Sunday (the best greeter you'd ever want) and helps by vacuuming the sanctuary, or whatever is needed. He knows everyone in town, and everyone knows and loves him. He's the most dedicated college baseball fan ever, perched shivering on the bleachers every February, huddled in his coat and hat, supporting every game of the season.

Joel has many friends, and some are typical, who come alongside in special ways. "The world moves much faster than Joel, but some of the baseball players appreciate him and stop once in a while and wait for him to catch up," Jessie said. Joel also takes one class a semester to build his strength and help his gait. "He's now taking kickboxing. Can you believe that?"

Some of Joel's friends are non-typical, like his friend Paul, who lives in an apartment building where most of the tenants are elderly. Paul brings them flowers, food, and whatever he thinks they need. Paul and Joel both reach out to others with unconditional love.

"Joel's the happiest and most fulfilled young man I know, and it's nothing we've done," Jessie said. "The Lord has opened each door for him, and Joel's walked through them. God brought people to enrich his life, beginning with us, his parents, as we met that plane landing from Korea, and the Lord still brings people into his life each day. We started our journey with his uneven gait, and now he walks all over town—filling each happy day."

Prayers answered.

Letters floating in your spoon:
F-O-R-E-V-E-R

And I will live in the house of the LORD forever.

—Psalm 23:6b NLT

Pieces of the Puzzle

Alone we can do so little; together we can do so much.

—Helen Keller

What do you think when you see a piece of a jigsaw puzzle? Is the puzzle almost finished, and this is the last piece (found under the table)? Or, is this the first piece, and the anticipation of hours hunched over the table thrills you?

If you're the family member of a child (or adult) on the autistic spectrum, a logo springs to mind. Why a puzzle piece for a logo? One person described it this way: "The beauty of a puzzle is all the pieces fit together and create a picture. All pieces are different. Your piece won't fit in my spot, nor will mine fit in your spot. All the pieces are important and we're all needed."

The interlocking, multicolored puzzle piece has become the international symbol of autism awareness. Its significance is multifaceted and the bright colors are said to represent hope. This hope is evident in Max Lucado's analogy: "We've been given only one piece of life's jigsaw puzzle. Only God has the cover of the box."

Afterword

See. I am doing a new thing!
Now it springs up; do you not perceive it?
I am making a way in the desert
and streams in the wasteland.

—Isaiah 43:19

Dear Reader,

You've picked up this book and you've taken your precious time to read it. We want you to know you've been prayed for on your challenging journey. Chapter One began with Proverbs 3:5–6 about trusting the Lord and him making our paths straight. There probably have been and are times—many times—on your path that you feel the sting of blowing sand in your eyes as you've trudged through your wilderness. The desert is a lonely place; just ask Moses in the Old Testament about his forty-year trek through the desert trying to lead a less-than-willing nation of refugees to the Promised Land. Moses wasn't alone; God had a plan.

Ask Jesus in the New Testament about enduring a forty-day fast, and then being tempted by Satan to turn stones into bread as his stomach clung to his ribs. Jesus wasn't alone; he knew God had a plan. Because Jesus didn't short-circuit God's plan, he took the difficult road from the desert, to the people he healed and loved, and then to the cross. Death. Silence. Deathly silence. Satan thought he had won. But Jesus' lonely journey here on Earth didn't stop there. His greatest miracle came after three days—he was alive!

Wildernesses and deserts are lonely. And our lives today can be lonely. However, we aren't alone, and God has a plan for your life. He is there and he is "new every morning." He was faithful to Moses, to Jesus, and to you.

So, these "afterwords" are words of encouragement, to let you know once again, "You're not alone."

Bibliography & Reading List

Chapman, Gary and Ross Campbell. *The Five Love Languages of Children.* Chicago, IL: Northfield Press, 2005.

Chapman, Gary. *The Five Love Languages of Teens.* Chicago, IL: Northfield Press, 2005.

_____. *The Five Love Languages: How to Express Heartfelt Commitment to Your Mate.* Chicago, IL: Northfield Press, 2004.

_____. *The Five Love Languages of God.* Chicago, IL: Northfield Publishing, 2002.

Colson, Emily. *Dancing with Max.* Grand Rapids, MI: Zondervan, 2010.

Hendrickson, Laura. *Finding Your Child's Way on the Autism Spectrum—Discovering Unique Strengths, Mastering Behavior Challenges.* Chicago, IL: Moody Publishers, 2009.

Kent, Carol. *Between a Rock and Grace Place; Divine Surprises in the Tight Spots of Life.* Grand Rapids, MI: Zondervan, 2010.

_____. *A New Kind of Normal, Hope-Filled Choices When Life Turns Upside-Down.* Nashville, TN: Thomas Nelson, 2007.

_____. *When I Lay My Isaac Down: Unshakable Faith in Unthinkable Circumstances.* Colorado Springs, CO: Navpress, 2004.

Kingsbury, Karen. *Unlocked—They Looked For A Miracle And Found It In A Song.* Grand Rapids, MI: Zondervan, 2010.

Langston, Kelly. *Autism's Hidden Blessings—Discovering God's Promises for Autistic Children & Their Families.* Grand Rapids, MI: Kregel Publications, 2009.

Lucado, Max. *God Came Near.* Nashville, TN: Thomas Nelson, 2004.

Myles, Brenda Smith and Richard L. Simpson. *Asperger Syndrome—A Guide For Educator And Parents* (second edition). Austin, TX: Pro-ed, Inc., 2003.

Owens, Connie S., Deborah White (illustrator). *Special Needs... Special Love—Relating to Children with Disabilities.* Anderson, IN: Warner Press, 2005.

Temple, Grandin. *Thinking in Pictures—My Life with Autism.* New York: Vintage Books, 2006.

Yancey, Philip. *Prayer: Does It Make Any Difference?* Grand Rapids, MI: Zondervan, 2006.

_____, *Reaching for the Invisible God, What Can We Expect To Find?* Grand Rapids, MI: Zondervan, 2000.

Glossary

ASD: Autism Spectrum Disorders. The term "spectrum" is crucial to understanding autism, because of the wide range of intensity, symptoms and behaviors, types of disorders, and as always, considerable individual variation. For further information, see pages 26-28.

ABA: Applied Behavioral Analysis. An early intervention technique for autism, in which skills are taught in small, more easily mastered steps.

Accommodations: Refers to the help that the law entitles a person with a developmental challenge to receive, to help them participate in school or society.

ADD, ADHD: Attention Deficit Disorder, Attention Deficit Hyperactivity Disorder. These are usually not considered to be on the spectrum, but they have some of the same behaviors, such as not being able to focus.

Asperger's Syndrome: A milder form of autism, characterized by significant difficulties in social situations. Some professionals say it should be a separate diagnosis from autism.

Aspie: A nickname for individuals with Asperger's Syndrome.

Aversion Therapy: A behavioral therapy term for negative consequences used to modify behavior.

BCBA: Board Certified Behavior Analyst. An autism treatment professional, possessing at least a master's degree, trained to analyze an autistic child's behavior.

Behavior Modification: Behavioral therapy is not a cure for autism, but rather a form of social training that makes it easier for children to function in the world around them. One of the simplest, yet most effective methods of functional behavioral assessment is called the "ABC" approach, where observations are made on Antecedents, Behaviors, and Consequences. In other words, "What comes directly before the behavior?" "What does the behavior look like?" and "What comes directly after the behavior?"

Drill: A behavioral term referring to a skill that is being taught in an ABA treatment program. Each repetition of the same drill is referred to as a trial.

Early Intervention: Treatment that teaches verbal and other skills that have not yet been acquired by an autism spectrum child and other children with special needs. Typically, it begins before age four and ends with entry into kindergarten.

Emergency Kit: Things carried in a tote when you go out with your child, such as items your child wants and needs, chews on, eats, drinks, or plays with depending on the age of your child. You can also carry the regular things you'd take in a diaper bag: Kleenex, wipes, a change of clothes. Add things for the caregiver, also.

Fade: After special assistance is given and a skill is mastered by child, fading is slowly withdrawing help.

Floor Time: Non-ABA early intervention technique. The most widely known dimension of floor time is following the child's lead, and harnessing the child's natural interests.

Inclusion: The degree to which an autism spectrum child is included in activities offered to general education students.

Information Card: A card with information about your child's condition to give to those who don't understand his or her behavior (in public).

Mainstream: A special education term used to describe a challenged child who attends regular classes with general education students, rather than in a special education classroom.

Meltdown: Trantrum-like behaviors that are more severe and last longer than "regular" tantrums.

Neurotypical: Typical; a non-spectrum person. Some use the term "normal," but what is normal?

Notebook: This may be a loose-leaf notebook with dividers you've made yourself, or apps for your iPhone, or a published resource such as *A Day At a Time*, a journal for parents of children with autism, by Jen Merheb. If you've scribbled and scratched over appointment times, cell phone numbers, school events, and the rest of your harried life on the myriad of calendars you possess, it may be time to get organized.

Your Notebook/Calendar/Journal might include the following dividers:

- Emergency numbers
- Any professionals working with your child (and/or your family)
- Daily log: What's happening and what happened with your child
- Medications, dosages, side effects, details
- Therapies

- Scripture
- Also add all the unique situations, people, helpful hints, and keeping-your-head-above-water sections you need

ODD: Oppositional Defiant Disorder is a chronic behavior disorder that disrupts a child's normal activities. Symptoms include the following:

- Throwing tantrums or arguing with parents or other adults
- Frequently refusing to comply with rules and requests
- Often blaming others for mistakes or misbehavior
- Often expressing hostility and seeking revenge
- Low frustration tolerance and easy loss of temper
- Treatment includes counseling and parent management training. Medication may be prescribed, especially if another condition, such as ADHD, is also present.

Processing: A neurological term describing the speed of brain functions. ASD children may have slower processing and trouble keeping up with social interactions and classroom activities.

Pullout: A special education student is "pulled out" of his regular class to attend therapy (speech, occupational, physical).

RDI: Relationship Development Intervention. A non-ABA early intervention treatment.

Redirect: Drawing a child away from an undesirable activity by capturing his attention with a new activity.

Reward: Positive consequence offered for successful performance of a drill. Can be faded once the new behavior is established.

Rituals and Insistence on Sameness:

- Routine to Ritual: Rigid adherence to a routine or activity carried out in a specific way, which then becomes a ritual or nonfunctional routine.
- Reactions with distress or tantrums to even small changes or disruptions in routines. Sometimes such reactions are so big they are described as catastrophic.
- Reflects difficulty with change in activities or routines or being able to predict what happens next. May be a *coping mechanism*.
- Repetitive movements with objects, such as lining things up, collecting objects, or clutching similar small toys. Repetitive and unusual movements with their body— mannerisms of the hands (such as hand-flapping, finger-twisting or flicking, rubbing, or wringing hands), body (such as rocking, swaying, or pacing), and odd posturing (such as posturing of the fingers, hands, arms, or toe-walking).
- Repetitive thoughts: Very strong interest in a particular kind of object (e.g., bugs, people's hair), parts of objects, or certain activities. These obsessions are persistent and intrusive. In young children, preoccupations with specific kinds of objects or actions, as well as repetitive thoughts about specific unusual topics, may be an early sign of obsessions.
- All these mannerisms may appear not to have any meaning or function; however, they may have significance for the child, such as providing sensory stimulation (also referred to as self-stimulating behavior, or "stimming"),

communicating to avoid demands, requesting a desired
object or attention, or soothing when anxious.

- Restricted patterns of interest refer to a limited range of
interests that are intense in focus. This may be particularly
apparent in very verbal children with autism or Asperger's
Syndrome who often become obsessed with a single topic
for months or even years. Restricted interests, obsessions,
and compulsions can interfere with a child's normal activity or social interaction, and can be related to anxiety. In
young children with ASD, similar restricted patterns may
be evident in repetitive movements with objects. Rather
than playing with toys in simple pretend play, or using
objects in appropriate ways, children with ASD line up or
stack toys or objects in the same way over and over again,
persistently knocking down and rolling objects, or wob-
bling or spinning objects, and they may show an intense
focus and interest in how these actions or objects look.

Shadowing: Watching a child to help when needed.

Social Stories: Social stories are short, carefully crafted stories written to help children (and adults) with autism navigate specific situations. In theory, they allow people to prepare for and rehearse social
interactions. It reduces anxiety, improves behavior, and helps set the
stage for building solid relationships.

Example: If your child feels alone, fearful, and dreads eating in
the school cafeteria, it doesn't do any good to tell him, "Eating in the
cafeteria is fun!" He knows it isn't, and you do, too. Just saying so
doesn't make it true. So, what do you do? Write down and use simple
sentences to walk him through these story steps.

- Who, what, where, and why does the situation occur? Your child needs these facts so he or she will recognize when the situation *does* occur. Directive sentences tell the child the appropriate social responses in that situation.
- Have your child describe his or her possible feelings or responses.
- Your child needs a sense of what others may be thinking or feeling in that situation. He or she lacks the ability to understand why others see, feel, and react differently than themselves. Write down what others may be thinking.
- Describe how other people will help out in a given situation.
- Have your child create sentences that help him or her remember strategies that work for your child. Your child will feel less frustrated, behave more typically, be more easily accepted, and feel better about himself or herself.

TEACH: Treatment and Education of Autistic and related Communication-Handicapped Children. Early intervention special education program in Chapel Hill, NC.

Resources

You-niquely Made Personality Study©

Using the You-niquely Made Personality Study can help you under-stand and appreciate family, friends, and others on your journey. All are uniquely made. Jot notes to jog your memory of how to best meet their needs—and your needs also.

Vibrant Yellow's sunshine can brighten your day, but too much can drain you dry. Sensitive Blue's rain clouds create beauty, but too many can dampen another's mood. Determined Red's instructions are helpful, but they can be overbearing. Calm Green's steadfast roots grow deep, but they can be unmovable.

This resource should help you see the bright side of each color's personality, and help you deal with each color's frailties. Remember that each color and combination (blend) has strengths and weaknesses. Some move, eat, and speak slowly, and some quickly. Some need people around constantly; others want to be alone. To some, everything is either right or wrong; others go with the flow.

Each color has different coping skills.

- The Yellow parent hits the wall but bounces back quickly and says, "Don't be so negative."

- The Blue parent (opposite from the Yellow) wants all the information given correctly and makes decisions slowly and thoroughly. "You can't make that decision off the top of your head," she says.
- The Red parent doesn't want details, rabbit trails, or an idea that fails. "We're going to beat this!"
- The Green parent (opposite from the Red) goes with the flow (as much as possible), listens, and when he is pressed to give an opinion, says, "Whatever they think is best."

Different factors drain and fill their emotional tanks. Developing appreciation for each gene color will improve your communication and relationships. Appreciation prevents you from taking anyone for granted. God designed us to communicate effectively with others and with him. He gave us his designer genes! King David said, "For you created my inmost being; you knit me together in my mother's womb. I praise you because I am fearfully and wonderfully made; your works are wonderful, I know that full well" (Ps. 139:13–14).

Vibrant Yellows

You hear Yellows before you see them—and continue to hear them, and hear them, and hear them. With high energy, they bounce into rooms, eyes sparkling, wearing a perpetual smile. They pounce and hug anyone in reach. They make Tigger look passive. To a Yellow, everyone is a best friend. They make those friends in elevators, standing in line at the grocery store, or answering a telemarketer's questions. Seldom wanting to be alone, they need "people fixes" often.

Yellows begin many things, but they finish few. They constantly hear the following refrains:

- "How can you live in all that clutter?"
- "Where are your keys?"
- "You got lost where? Again?"

What drains their emotional tanks? Being alone and having to finish anything carefully (not simply slapping it together). How do they react when their emotional tanks register empty? They talk more and louder. (Their opposites—the Blues—can't imagine that Yellows can talk more or louder.) If that doesn't work, they get totally quiet, and everyone says, "What's wrong with her, she's so quiet?"

How do you fill Yellow's emotional tank? You fill it with people, by giving them time, talk, and touch (many hugs). You can also help them with organization. So, how do Yellows fill others' tanks? They brighten a room. We can all use the warmth they give, especially on dreary days.

Snapshot: When Yellow Brightened a Dreary Day

As Diane walked wearily from the parking garage to the hospital, her mind was preoccupied with her daughter's serious surgery.

"Well, hi there!" a tiny voice interrupted.

She looked around, then down. There stood a small, smiling boy. His father stood behind him, locking the car.

"Hi there," Diane replied.

"What you doin' here?"

"I'm visiting my daughter. She's sick."

"I'm gonna see my nana," the boy said and rapidly shot the details. His father sighed and said, "Son, leave the lady alone."

"Oh, that's okay."

The boy continued his story, as the father repeated, "Son, leave the lady alone."

To please the dad, Diane said, "I need to get on in. You have a good day." A few seconds later, Diane was approaching the hospital door.

"Well, hi there," she heard the same boy say to a lady getting out of her car. "What you doin' here?"

"Son, leave the lady alone."

Inside the hospital, as she headed down the gray corridor, Diane smiled. "Thank you, Lord. I really needed that little ray of sunshine!"

Helpful Hints if You're a Yellow

Yellows have trouble focusing, especially on things they don't want to do. The result? Things pile up and they feel overwhelmed. Yellows, focus on the first and most important task you need to do. Finish that before you go to the second. To do that, you may need to take small bites of the elephant. The task you've been putting off may look like an elephant, so remember this: you can't eat an elephant at one sitting. In the same way, you can't complete a huge task quickly. You have to take small bites—tackle small parts of the job. Here's a helpful hint if you find you can't stay at a task for a long time. Set a timer for fifteen minutes. You can do almost anything for that length of time. Take small bites, do parts of big task, and be thankful for what you accomplish.

Now, what's that task you've put off? Cleaning a bathroom floor covered with dirty clothes and wet towels? Filing medical, educational, and/or psychological papers and overdue bills? Finding your keys—again? Get started—not after one more computer game, telephone call, or email excuse.

If you're a Yellow, you have to take the time to make a home for everything. Once you accomplish that task and put things back in their place—each time—it will become a habit. You'll put the dirty clothes and towels in the hamper, the mail in a certain stack (a shoebox will work), and the keys back on the hook. Surprisingly, you'll be able to find items when you need them and save yourself valuable time and frustration.

Give Thanks for Yellows

Who are the Yellows in your life? Jot down their names and tell them thanks—they'll probably do even more. Even weary Yellows spread sunshine. Here are a few things to be thankful for in the Yellows you know:

> Keep your eyes open for those bright rays—whatever their size.

- Continual contagious smile
- Hugs
- Friendliness, which is especially important to others who may be shy
- High energy level when others are winding down
- Click with children

Be thankful for those lights shining in the darkness.

Sensitive Blues

You've met the high-energy, talkative, outgoing Yellows. They multi-task, start many projects, and finish few. Although their rollercoaster emotions zoom from tears to laughter, they still "go with the flow" as situations change. They see their glass as at least half-full or overflowing as they spread their optimistic sunshine.

Who are the Blues? In contrast to the Yellows, they're low-energy, quiet introverts. They do one thing at a time, slowly, and stay with it until it's completed perfectly. Their emotions, accompanied by sighing, register on two levels—deep and deeper. Blues don't like to go with the flow because transitions are traumatic. They need time to process the changes, and the new spectrum journey is packed with overwhelming transitions.

They see their glass as half-empty—and draining. "Our half-empty glass is how the world really is," said a Blue. "At least we see things in an objective way."

We need Blue's devotion to detail, to jobs done well—such as balancing the checkbook to the penny—even if it takes them hours to do so. Blues correctly fill out medical, educational, and/or psychological papers and meticulously place them in folders.

Blues seriously think through situations, ponder, and in time give you their answer. People turn to them because they know Blues genuinely care. They read people well but sometimes read into situations more than is there. When overwhelmed in a crisis, pushed to hurry up, or deprived of time alone, their emotional tanks empty rapidly. They may become worn out, depressed, or simply shut down. As things build inside, an explosion may eventually erupt, leaving others confused. "What's wrong with her? She never acts like that, she's usually so quiet." If you're a Blue, you need to share what's going on. Let people know how you feel. No one can read your mind.

How do you fill Blues' emotional tanks? Give them lots of solitary time in a space of their own—away from crowds and noise—so they can process information. They live by their own time schedule and their way of doing things. Since transitions are traumatic, alert them to coming changes and give them time to adjust.

Who usually marry each other? Many times, it is opposite Yellows and Blues. Notice the totally different needs in Yellows and Blues. What helps one probably won't help the other; communication is desperately needed.

While on this challenging journey, we especially need Blue's sympathy, hugs, and organizational skills.

Snapshot: Blue to the Rescue

"How's your wife doing?" Yellow Roy's voice boomed across the room.

"I got her home from the hospital Wednesday," the weary husband answered.

Roy slapped him on the back. "Well, that's great!" he said while looking around the room.

The husband continued, "But I'm not sure where we go from here..."

"Uh huh," Roy replied, as he spotted his next encounter and headed off, adding his standard, "I'll be praying for you."

That's the picture. Yellow playing Duck, Duck, Goose, touching people as he continued in circles, not recognizing the deep need standing before him.

Then, up walked Blue Dave, slipping his arm around the weary husband's shoulders. "Claude, how's Jenny doing?"

As Claude related the last week's journey and the uncertainty of the tomorrows, Dave listened. He made Claude feel as if he were the only person in the room.

"I'm so sorry you're going through this. May I come by this afternoon and we'll talk?"

Noticing Claude's eyes brim with tears, Dave continued, "Can I pray with you right now?"

> Blues quietly wrap around hurting people, giving support.

Helpful Hints if You're a Blue

Life is a process, not perfection. Your halfway effort will be better than almost everyone else's best tries, so don't procrastinate because you feel you have to attempt perfection.

Appreciate all that the different colors have to offer. You have deep feelings for others and take on their hurts, especially on this difficult journey. However, you may feel that optimistic Yellows aren't serious enough, driven Reds don't care enough, and passive Greens don't show enough emotion.

Pray for acceptance and appreciation of others. We're all in this together and desperately need each other.

Give Thanks for Blues

Who are they in your life? Jot down their names and tell them thanks. They will appreciate your thoughtfulness.

Here are a few things to be thankful for in the Blues you know:

- Feel deeply
- Support friends no matter what
- Organize everything
- Manage money (this journey needs that quality)
- Analyze decisions carefully

Be thankful for sensitive Blue genes.

Determined Reds

Fasten your seatbelt—here come the Reds. They know what needs to be done, how to do it, and they want it done now. They demand the bottom line (of whatever is happening) and don't care about details. Just get it done, and then move on to the next task. Reds persevere no matter the obstacles and can't understand why everyone else doesn't do the same. "I walked around on a broken leg for a week; she's complaining about a sprained ankle," stated a Red.

Two Reds together? They both think they're right. In a face off, they wait for the other to realize it. "You should have seen the standoff between my child and her preschool teacher. I wasn't sure which one would win. It changed from day to day," said a mom.

They keep people's feet to the fire, not cutting them slack, while working circles around everyone. So do they need their emotional tanks filled? Yes, whether they realize it or not. You can tell when they're on empty; they get louder and more demanding. If that doesn't work, they get totally quiet, and everyone then waits for the other shoe to drop.

How do you fill a Red's tank? Give them appreciation for what they do—that's how they show love. Saying something like, "Thanks for all your hard work getting this information and getting the job done," is music to their ears. Also, don't give them details, stay off rabbit trails, and simply give the bottom line. When the going gets rough, or, if you simply need a guide, you need a Red.

Snapshot: A Trip to NYC

At a New York City hotel, a Red mom unpacked suitcases and said to her husband and daughter (both Blue-Greens), "I've made an agenda so we can make the best use of our time."

Dad and daughter smiled and rolled their eyes at each other.

"Mom, can I just rest for a few minutes?" moaned the teenager.

"We don't want to waste this weekend in the room."

"Do we have to walk everywhere?"

"Of course not. The subway's right across the street. Let's go."

The three headed out, agenda clutched in mom's hand. She walked briskly and spoke into the air, "Isn't this great!" Her husband and daughter knew the answer they were to give but were busy trying to keep up the pace. They raced down the steep stairs leading to the subway. Mom stopped to check the subway map.

"Why do you want to look at this? You've got it all planned out," said her husband.

"It's fun to see where we are on the map and where we're going." She traced her finger along the color-coded routes, "Let's try this other line and see if we can cut off some stops."

"Mom, we're gonna get lost."

"Of course we won't. Besides, this is an adventure."

"Does the adventure include going back to the room this afternoon?"

"You really want to do that?"

"Can't I just rest for a little while?"

"OK, but you'll miss all the afternoon."

"That's okay, Mom."

Backtracking to the hotel, daughter was left to rest and read. She was happy.

Mom hit the pavement in full stride, checking off her list. She was happy.

Dad attempted keeping up with mom. We think he was happy, but we know he was exhausted. Back home, two days later, mom announced, "Wasn't that a great trip!"

"Uh huh," they answered.

Two months later, dad and daughter looked through the trip pictures again. "You know, that was fun," said dad.

"Yeah, but don't tell Mom."

Both smiled and rolled their eyes.

Helpful Hints if You're a Red

Stop, look, and listen:

- Stop—or at least slow down. You're used to telling others to stop, now do so yourself.
- Look—at others in the eye, not above their shoulder or at your watch.
- Listen—to what others say.

- Keep your opinions (how others could do things better) to yourself, unless asked. When you do speak the truth, do it in love. Be tactfully truthful. Give your time, attention, and encouragement as gifts to others. They respect your opinion, especially if you've done the previous three steps.

Give Thanks for Reds

Who are they in your life? Jot down their names and tell them thanks—if you can catch them. Here are a few things to be thankful for in the Reds you know:

> Reds organize, prioritize, and best yet, they persevere. That's especially needed on this journey.

- High energy, when others wind down
- Objectively see the big picture—what needs to be done and how to do it—and give the bottom line
- Tenaciously persevere until a task is completed
- Keep self and others on task (hold feet to the fire)
- Excel in a crisis ("He just lives for times like this," is usually said of a Red)

Be thankful for those who shout, "Stop. I can help."

Calm Greens

Now sit back and relax. Can you hear the soothing sound of a porch swing clicking back and forth and back and forth? That's the sound of the go-with-the-flow, predictable Greens. Emotionally, they have no highs and no lows. They're great in a crisis. They get along with almost everyone. Greens go through life in slow motion—whether walking, talking, or eating. This pace drives Reds crazy. "When I tell her to hurry, she slows down!" Reds and Greens are two more opposites who may end up marrying each other.

Greens don't demand attention, so they can be easily overlooked. Of growing up in a household with more demanding siblings, a Green once said, "I felt invisible at the dinner table with my two brothers who hogged all the attention." Teachers may not remember the names of their Green students because they're busy keeping up with the Reds and Yellows bouncing around the room.

Green's emotional tank drains slowly, but it does drain—especially when alone time becomes packed with people and activities. They become quieter, finally digging in their heels, not budging. Since they've gone along with everyone before, people are surprised at this reaction. "I told him we're going out to dinner, and he just sat there reading the paper. He wouldn't move!" stated a Red wife.

How do you fill these easygoing emotional tanks? "You mean, he really needs something?" asked his wife. Yes, and since Greens don't demand attention, hearing their name or appreciation for what they've done will fill their tanks quickly. Remember their low energy level; they live for a good nap. Let them have one. Greens are low-key, undemanding children who passively enter a low-key, undemanding adulthood.

Snapshot: Teacher's Lounge, 1984

"I'm so relieved they didn't laugh him off the stage." My teacher colleague was telling us about the speaker at her son's Ivy League college graduation that past weekend. "I watched as he sauntered up to the podium, smiled at the graduating class, and then he started singing: 'It's a beautiful day in the neighborhood . . . '

"I held my breath, as those unresponsive seniors stared silently at the stage. Then, during the song, they slowly melted into swaying three-year-olds, leaning forward on their folding chairs. They even joined in singing his song. He had them in the palm of his hand. I can't remember what he said, just how he said it. Then, as he closed, they jumped to their feet clapping, whistling, and the girls rushed the stage shoving programs for his autograph.

"They yelled, 'Remember me?' I guess they thought he'd seen them through the TV set years ago." All of us smiled and nodded as she continued.

"And, I loved all those sophisticated seniors shouting, 'Get my picture with my best friend, Mr. Rogers.' He just patiently stood there smiling with those kids as flashbulbs kept going off."

As a young child, extremely shy Fred Rogers was encouraged by his Grandfather McFeely. Fred became the famous Mr. Rogers, encouraging generations through unconditional love.

Helpful Hints if You're a Green

Procrastination may be a familiar problem to you. Yellows procrastinate because they take on too much; Greens procrastinate because they use lack of energy as their excuse. Like Yellows, you need to take small bites of the elephant (see the helpful hints for Yellows). Greens need to focus, especially to finish tasks. You should also speak up and give feedback. Don't be prideful, saying, "No one knows what I'm thinking." It's counterproductive. Also, others need your input to help make decisions. You have a balanced outlook. Yes, even Reds need it.

Give Thanks for Greens

Who are they in your life? Jot down their names and be sure to thank them—by name. Here are a few things to be thankful for in the Greens you know:

> Greens give unconditional love, accepting you just as you are. See things objectively.

- Sit and listen, don't interrupt
- Go with the flow; act rather than react

- Create calmness in crisis
- Reliable

Be thankful for relaxed Green genes.

Ways We Give and Receive Love

Dovetailing with color-coded personalities is the understanding of how others give and receive love, taken from Gary Chapman's book *The Five Love Languages: Ways You Give and Receive Love*. Chapman's books have strengthened families and influenced countless relationships. More information on his books is given in Resource Four.

Who needs what, in your family, to refill those empty emotional tanks? According to Chapman's book, love is given and received in five primary languages:

- Talk: "Let me hear something positive. I need to know I'm doing something right."
- Touch: Babies thrive on it; children feel special with it; teens may not acknowledge it, but they desire a passing nudge; adults sometimes admit, "I just need a hug."
- Time: "Just sit down and spend time with me. Don't be glancing at your watch."
- Gifts: "I can't believe my sister gave me a little shell from last summer's trip. And, you know, gifts don't have to cost anything—it's just important that someone thinks about you in a tangible way. Also, I can glance at the shell and relive the moment for a long time."
- Deeds: "OK, so you say, 'I love you,' a lot. When you pick your wet towels up off the floor and hang them up, I'll know you mean it. Actions speak louder than words."

"My wife 'speaks' three of the love languages, and I speak the other two. Amazing we communicate at all," a husband said and laughed.

Which languages are important to you? How about others in your family? Talk it over and each week have everyone write down one thing they need. As the family meets each other's emotional needs, everyone wins. Pray for the willingness and follow-through to give these gifts—when it is easy and when it is not so easy.

The "-Ists" List—Therapists and Specialists

The following specialized professionals may help you on your journey.

Developmental Pediatrician: If you have a child who is or may be diagnosable on the spectrum, you may be referred to a developmental pediatrician, who has specialized training.

Speech-Language Pathologist:
- They evaluate and treat disorders of speech, language, voice, and feeding/swallowing.
- Non-verbal communication. This may include teaching gestural communication, or training with PECs (picture exchange cards), electronic talking devices, and other non-verbal communication tools.
- It's all well and good to know how to say "Good morning," but it's just as important to know when, how, and to whom you should say it.
- Conversation skills. Knowing how to make statements is not the same thing as carrying on conversations. Speech

therapists may work on back-and-forth exchange and capturing joint attention, which leads to turn-taking skills.

- They are useful for normalizing hyper- or hyposensitivities to foods to which the child has texture, temperature, or other aversions.

Behavior Specialists: When a person with autism displays challenging or violent behaviors, a behavior specialist may be recommended.

Play Therapists: "A child's play is his 'work,' and the 'toys' are his words," says Dr. Gary Landreth, a noted play therapist. How much more so for an SC whose "work" and "words" need extra help? Thus, play therapy. Play therapy is something akin to Floor-Time Therapy, a play-based technique that builds on the SC's own interests or obsessions to develop relationships and social/communication skills. This interaction helps the child relate to others in ordinary ways. Autism is largely a social-communication disorder. Children with autism find it extremely difficult to relate to others—particularly to peers—in ordinary ways. A typical child would pick up a baby doll and say, "My baby," instead of being self-absorbed with an object. Very often, too, play therapy can allow parents to take an active role in their child's growth and development. Play therapy can be taught to parents and, over time, parents can become their child's therapist, while also building a stronger, more meaningful relationship.

Physical Therapists: Autism is a pervasive developmental disorder. This means that most people on the autism spectrum have delays, differences, or disorders in many areas, including gross and fine motor skills. Children on the spectrum may have low muscle tone, or have a tough time with coordination and sports. These issues can interfere with basic day-to-day functioning, and they're almost certain to interfere with social and physical development. Physical therapists may work with very young children on basic motor skills, such as sitting, rolling, standing, and playing. They may also work with parents to teach them some techniques for helping their child build muscle strength, coordination, and skills.

As children grow older, physical therapists are more likely to come to a child's preschool or school. There, they may work on more sophisticated skills, such as skipping, kicking, throwing, and catching. These skills are not only important for physical development, but also for social engagement in sports, recess, and general play.

In school settings, physical therapists may pull children out to work with them one on one, or "push in" to typical school settings, such as gym class, to support children in real-life situations. It's not unusual for a physical therapist to create groups including typical and autistic children to work on the social aspects of physical skills. Physical therapists may also work with special education teachers and aides, gym teachers, and parents to provide tools for building social/physical skills.

Physical therapists (often called "PTs") are trained to work with people to build or rebuild strength, mobility, and motor skills. Some help children and adults who are coping with lifelong disabilities such as cerebral palsy, or related neurological disabilities.

Dance and movement therapy, hippotherapy (therapeutic horseback riding), aquatic therapy (therapeutic swimming), recreational therapy, and even play therapy may also be offered by people with a background in physical therapy. While none of these specialized services is likely to be supported by medical insurance, many may be right for your child. Some of these therapies are beginning to be covered, though. You should talk to the professional and ask if they have experience in medical report writing that might allow them to submit for these activities.

Occupational Therapists (OT): Occupational therapists have vastly expanded the historical breadth of their job. In the past, for example, an occupational therapist might have worked with an autistic person to develop skills for handwriting, shirt-buttoning, shoe-tying, and so forth. But today's occupational therapists specializing in autism may also be experts in sensory integration (difficulty with processing information through the senses), or they may work with their clients on play skills and more.

Since people with autism often lack some of the basic social and personal skills required for independent living, occupational therapists have developed techniques for working on all of these needs. For example:

- Provide interventions to help a child appropriately respond to information coming through the senses. Intervention may include swinging, brushing, playing in a ball pit, or a whole gamut of other activities aimed at helping a child better manage his body in space.
- Facilitate play activities that instruct as well as aid a child in interacting and communicating with others. For the OT specializing in autism, this can translate specifically into structured play therapies, such as Floor-Time, which were developed to build intellectual and emotional skills, as well as physical skills.
- Devise strategies to help the individual transition from one setting to another, from one person to another, and from one life phase to another. For a child with autism, this may involve soothing strategies for managing transition from home to school; for adults with autism, it may involve vocational skills, cooking skills, and more.

- Develop adaptive techniques and strategies to get around apparent disabilities (for example, teaching keyboarding when handwriting is simply impossible; selecting a weighted vest to enhance focus).

Music and Art Therapists: These therapists create avenues for children to express themselves through these media, exploring expression through musical activities or through mixed art media.

Organizations, Websites, and Government Resources

Resource Organizations

American Occupational Therapy Association (AOTA)
www.aota.org
Occupational Therapist play a key role in strategies and techniques helping with social interactions, school performance, and safety.

American Physical Therapy Association (APTA)
www.apta.org
For children, occupational therapists assist in play, school, and daily living, such as the balance of "too much, too little" on swings, climbing apparatus and unstable surfaces as children learn to adapt. Sensory Integration is active not passive—the child does it and sees the results. They are problem solving—with the therapist being a guide and observer.

American Speech-Language-Hearing Association (ASHA)
www.asha.org
This organization is the professional association for 140,000 audiologists, speech-language pathologists, and speech, language, and hearing scientists.

Autism Society of America
www.autism-society.org
This site offers a wealth of information, including a directory of

local chapters, current research and e-newsletter, programs and support, daily tips, and even a list of sensory friendly films.

Autism Speaks
www.autismspeaks.org
The Autism Speaks site disseminates information about legislation that relates to autism and how to become involved on the local level. Autism Speaks is the nation's largest autism science and advocacy organization, dedicated to funding research into the causes, prevention, treatments, and a cure for autism; increasing awareness of autism spectrum disorders; and advocating for the needs of individuals with autism and their families.

Families for Early Autism Treatment (FEAT)
www.feat.org
FEAT is a nonprofit organization of parents, educators, and other professionals dedicated to providing world-class education, advocacy, and support for the family.

National Autism Association
www.NationalAutismAssociation.org
The mission of the National Autism Association is to respond to the most urgent needs of the autism community, providing real help and hope so that all affected can reach their full potential. This is a resource of many helpful links.

Sociable Kidz
www.sociablekidz.com
Sociable Kidz is a social skills group for kids from preschool (age four) through eighth grade taught by two classroom teachers. Their mission is to take practical daily techniques used in classrooms and use them in Sociable Kidz sessions. They are constantly working on improving children's self-esteem. They focus daily on problem-solving strategies, as well as teaching kids how to make friends, how to make eye contact, and how to share.

Web Sites/Blogs

Autism Support Network
www.AutismSupportNetwork.com
Thousands of families share what works, coping strategies, and life guides on their daily journey.

The Autistic Touch

www.theautistictouch.com
This blog by Mary Donachy is about life with her granddaughter, Jenny. He story is listed in Chapter Three.

Colleen Swindoll-Thompson Blog

www.insightforliving.typepad.com/specialneeds.
Colleen Swindoll-Thompson is the daughter of Chuck Swindoll and has a wonderful blog for special-needs families. She has an autistic son, and part of her story is in Chapter Nine of this book.

Emily Colson Blog

www.emilycolson.com
Emily Colson is the daughter of Chuck Colson. The story of her son, Max, and his grandfather is in printed in Chapter Nine. She is an artist and writer. After many years as an art and creative director in the field of advertising and design, she now pours her creative gifts into helping her son, Max, who is diagnosed with autism. She has even pioneered an innovative communication system to assist her son. Emily has been a single mother for most of Max's twenty years, with hard-fought lessons of life, love, and laughter. Emily has a terrific blog on her website, and her book, *Dancing with Max*, is listed in the Bibliography.

Joni and Friends

www.joniandfriends.org
Joni and Friends reaches out to special need families. The website contains information and DVD on autism and church.

MOM—NOS (Mom—not otherwise specified)

momnos.blogspot.com
Written by a mom who helps the rest of us "get it." Her blog on 3/13/10 is so helpful in appreciating the same-and-different brains of typical and ASD people. It was given to her child's fourth grade class, but helps adults too. It's called, "On being a hair-dryer kid in a toaster world."

SibNet

www.siblingsupport.org
SibNet is a website for siblings of special needs persons.

Tim Tucker Blog

www.bothhandandflashlight.com
Tim Tucker writes Both Hands and a Flashlight, a blog for parents whose children are or may be on the autism spectrum. "We

believe there's nothing 'wrong' with any of our children. They are just striving to overcome many challenges, and they are perfect just as they are. This is a 'come-as-you-are' kind of blog, where the spectrum of emotions is welcome. We aren't super-parents; we're human. We believe the pursuit of becoming the best parents we can is what matters. We believe in the adventure. We believe in never giving up. We believe in advocating fiercely for our children. And first and foremost, we believe in them."

Government Resources

The CDC's Autism Information Center
www.cdc.gov/ncbddd/autism/
This site informs about CDC and congressional activity; resources for families, educators, and practitioners; publications and databases.

National Institute of Mental Health
www.nimh.nih.gov/health/topics/autism-spectrum-disorders-pervasive-developemntal-disorders/index.shtml
NIMH offers science news, ASD publications, NIH activities, and more.

US Department of Health & Human Services
www.acf.hhs.gov/programs/add/
DHHS provides original documentation on government programs and findings. Entering the keyword "autism" in the search function for this site will result in numerous links to autism-related topics on the site.

About the Author

Lynda Young is cofounder of Kindred Spirits International. Through conferences, books, publications, and ministries, KSI outreaches include children's hospitals, women's groups, the medical community, and Amani ya Juu, a refugee women's mission in Nairobi, Kenya. A member of the American Association of Christian Counselors, Lynda is a nationwide speaker and an award-winning author/writer. She continually shares her passion for helping others "come alongside" families who are hurting when their children are suffering. She holds masters degrees in religious education from the Southwestern Baptist Theological Seminary and education/administration from the University of North Carolina. Her work includes positions as a teacher/administrator, and she has published and taught You-niquely Made© curricula on personalities. She holds memberships in the American Christian Writers and Advanced Writers and Speakers Associations. She is also a graduate of Speak Up with Confidence and CLASSeminars.

Lynda's first book in the You Are Not Alone series, *Hope for Families of Children with Cancer*, won the Living Now Silver book Award: parenting category. Her second book, *Hope for Families of Children with Congenital Heart Defects*, was finalist in the National "Best Books" Award: parenting/family category. Lynda continues her writing in this series to encourage parents of children with chronic conditions.

Lynda and her husband, Dr. John L. Young, have four children, eleven grandchildren, and four great-grandchildren. Her husband has been in cancer research statistics on a national and international level since 1965, and he is a professor at Emory University. The live in Snellville, Georgia, and are active at Annistown Road Baptist Church.